4- and 8-bit Microprocessors, Architecture and History

Patrick H. Stakem

© 2013

3rd edition

Number 1 in the
Computer Architecture series

Introduction

This book surveys the history and architecture of 8-bit microprocessors. We actually start with a look at a strange 1-bit processor, look at 4-bits and 8-bits, then 12 bit micros. The 16-bit processors are the subject of another book in this series. Four and eight bit processors are still manufactured and used. This book is not an exhaustive view of the field, but the major players are covered.

There is a brief review of computer architecture, binary math, and digital logic that you can skip, if you are familiar with these topics.

The evolution of the 8-bit processors is a history of the advance of semiconductor technology from the first transistors, to the breakthrough of multiple transistors on a chip, the integrated circuit. A lot of this happened when the "Silicon Valley" of northern California was mostly known for its citrus crops. The tools that made all this happen were large mainframe computers with vacuum tube technology, punched card input, and memory drums with the staggering capacity of a thousand words. The growth of the integrated circuit shows what Gordon Moore observed was an exponential growth law: the complexity increased about every 18 months. Naturally, this growth rate is not sustainable forever. But, in the age of multi-core 64-bit microprocessor systems on a chip, so far, so good.

The figure of merit or metric used for a chip's complexity is the number of transistors incorporated in the chip. This makes some sense, because a transistor is a switching element, and the complexity is related to the number of switching elements. Another figure of merit is the number of (logic) gates, which can use a transistor or two. This is all like the rating of a car's engine in horsepower, even though there's no horse. Back when steam engines were being developed, engineers related to the number of horses they could replace.

What is an 8-bit processor, anyway? In general, we consider the width of the registers and arithmetic logic unit, the internal data bus width. The external data bus may be different. The width of the address bus may also be larger than the word size. There are exceptions to the rules.
An 8-bit processor can handle 16-bit data, even floating point data.

Complexity has to go somewhere. There are a certain minimum numbers of things the processor has to do. Implementing these in hardware makes the device more complex, and harder to manufacture and test. Moving some of the complexity to software will work, but then requires more memory resources.

The author

The author built an Intel 8080-based Altair 8800 computer in 1975. He went to the Big Computer Faire in Atlantic City, and saw two guys, both named Steve, from California, with a wooden-cased project that probably wasn't going to go anywhere commercially. His Aerospace career has revolved around support for space-based microprocessors and computers for NASA since 1971.

Mr. Stakem received a Bachelor's Degree in Electrical Engineering from Carnegie Mellon University, and masters in Physics and Computer Science from the Johns Hopkins University. He has followed a career as a NASA support contractor, working at every NASA Site. He was associated with the Graduate Computer Science Department at Loyola University in Maryland, the Whiting School of Engineering of the Johns Hopkins University, and Capital Institute of Technology.

Pictures are from the author's collection, unless otherwise noted. Many thanks to John Culver of cpushack.com for information, assistance, and pictures. Special thanks to J. Chris Hausler for his sanity check on my Motorola discussion.

Mr. Stakem can be found on Facebook and Linkedin.

Computer Architecture

A *computer* performs arithmetic and logic functions on data, and provides flow of control. The arithmetic functions we would like to have performed are additional, subtraction, multiplication, and division. Actually, as we will see later, if we can subtract, we can do any of these operations. Multiplication can merely be repeated addition. The logical operations on binary data include inversion, AND, OR, Exclusive OR, and derivative functions such as Negated-AND (NAND), Negated-OR (NOR), and Negated-exclusive OR (NXOR). Actually, for two binary symbols, there are 16 possible functions. Only some of these have names (and are useful). As with the mathematical functions, some can be represented as combinations of others. We'll look at mathematical and logical functions applied to binary data, and how the mathematical functions can be expressed in terms of the logical ones.

The *Von Neuman Architecture* says there is no distinction between the code and the data. This was an observation by John von Neumann of the Institute for Advanced Studies at Princeton University. While consulting for the Moore School of Electrical Engineering at the University of Pennsylvania, von Neumann wrote an incomplete "First Draft of a Report on the EDVAC" (computer). The paper described a computer architecture in which the data and the program are both stored in the computer's memory in the same address space. Before this, it was the custom to have separate code and data storage (the Harvard architecture), and they were not necessarily the same size or format. Von Neumann observed that the code is also data. Most modern microprocessors are this style. For speed, especially in digital signal processors, designers revert to the older *Harvard* architecture, with separate code and data stores, as this gives a speed-up in accessing from memory. In Harvard architecture, it is difficult to have self-modifying code, which is a good thing from the debugging standpoint.

The fetch/execute cycle

This section discusses how an instruction gets executed. The basic process is referred to as the *fetch/execute cycle*. First the instruction is fetched from memory, and then the instruction is executed, which can involve the fetching and writing of data items.

Instructions are executed in steps called *machine cycles*. Each machine cycle might take several machine clock times to complete. If the architecture is pipelined, then each machine cycle consists of a stage in the pipeline. At each step, a memory access or an internal operation (ALU operation) is performed. Machine cycles are sequenced by a state machine in the CPU logic, driven by a clock source.

A register called the *program counter* contains the location in memory of the next instruction to be executed. The contents of the program counter get automatically updated as the instruction executes. The address of the next instruction to be executed (not necessarily the next adjacent instruction) is put in the program counter. A *register* is a temporary holding memory for data, and is part of the CPU. At initialization time (boot), the program counter is loaded with the location of the first instruction to be executed. After that, it is simply incremented, unless there is a change in the flow of control, such as a branch or jump. In this case, the target address of the branch or jump is put into the program counter.

The first step of the instruction execution is to fetch the instruction from memory into a special holding location called the *Instruction Register*. At this point, the instruction is decoded, meaning a control unit figures out, from the bit pattern, what the instruction is to do. This control unit implements the *ISA*, the instruction set architecture. Without getting too complicated, we could have a flexible control unit that could execute different ISA's. That's possible, but beyond the scope of our discussion here.

With the instruction decode complete, the machine knows what resources are required for instruction execution. A typical math instruction, for example, would require two data reads from memory, an

Arithmetic Logic Unit (ALU) operation, and a data write. The data items might be in registers, or memory.

The ISA for a processor defines its basic machine language instructions. Each machine language instruction maps into one or more microinstructions in the control unit. The software view of the CPU is the ISA. If we want to program the CPU, we write a series of machine code instructions. We got a pad, a pencil, a list of the instructions, and a schematic of the CPU. Trust me when I say this was a complicated, error-prone, difficult task. There were no tools to help. The chip manufacturers manipulated silicon, and didn't get into the software business. Hardware engineers were used to wiring something together and getting it to work. They didn't see the point of "software."

But, eventually, early programmers coded up (manually) a useful tool, called the assembler. It could translate a higher-level abstracted view of the processor into machine language, and do the bookkeeping on resources. Major advances, higher level languages such as FORTRAN and COBOL, were in the future. Other tools were developed to prepare the machine code for implementation in a ROM. Things were looking up. Of course, you kept your machine language program written neatly on a lined pad. Electronic storage? What electronic storage?

If you actually wanted to solve a real problem, assembly language was not an easy solution. The first BASIC compiler allowed one to approach the problem solution from an algebraic and procedural point of view. But, it abstracted away the underlying hardware details. In theory, a BASIC program for one machine could be re-compiled for another, and be expected to work.

Let's go back a second to an even more obscure topic in machine programming, the microcode. We said that machine instructions were translated into a series of steps (think, fetch-execute) that the CPU preformed. A fetch was a memory read of the instruction. An execute operation could involve operand fetches, various logical and math operations, and possibly a memory write of the results. Status flags need to be set. Interrupts need to be tended to. The state machine of the instruction decoder/controller unit is complex. If it is hard-wired logic, there's nothing we can do to change it. BUT, if the instruction decode and execution sequencing is controlled by a ROM memory look-up, well…. we can change the response of the controller to an instruction's bit pattern. If we dare. Actually, this is useful for the designers, who understand the ALU logic, in fixing problems, and adding features. The base instruction set might be implemented in ROM, with some associated PROM to hold updates and fixes. If we go way over the top, we might have the ability to change the structure of the ALU as well. That's a topic for FPGA's; and we won't go into it here. So, could you write in microcode, and develop new instructions? Why, yes you could. This was done on the IBM mainframes. In fact, the floppy disk resulted from a need to input microcode changes to the hardware.

Logical operations on data

Logical operations are done on a bit-by-bit basis. There is no interaction between adjacent bit positions.

The Unary function, (function of 1 variable) is "negate". This changes a 0 to a 1, or a 1 to a 0. There is one input, and one output.

There are 16 possible binary functions (function of 2 input variables). These include AND, OR, and XOR, and their negations, NAND, NOR, and NXOR. The other 10 don't have specific names.

$$C = f(A,B)$$

.Elementary Binary Math operations

The elementary math operations include add, subtract, multiply, divide.

The laws of binary addition

0+0=0
1+0=1
0+1=1
1+1=0 (with a carry)

<u>Laws of binary subtraction</u> (Remember a-b does not equal b-a)

0-0=0
0-1=1 (with a borrow)
1-0=1
1-1=0

<u>Laws of binary multiplication</u>

0 x 0 = 0
0 x 1 = 0
1 x 0 = 0
1 x 1 = 1

(That's easy; anything times 0 is 0)

<u>Laws of binary division</u>

(Division by zero is not defined. There is no answer.)

0 / 0 = not allowed
1 / 0 = not allowed
0 / 1 = 0
1 / 1 = 1

Math in terms of logic functions

Here, we see that mathematical functions can be implemented by logical operations. That's good, because microelectronics implements logical functions. George Boole worked out the theoretical basis of this in the middle 1800's.

Addition

+		half-add	carry	
0	0	0	0	$0 + 0 = 0$
0	1	1	0	$0 + 1 = 1$
1	0	1	0	$1 + 0 = 1$
1	1	0	1	$1 + 1 = 0$, with a carry (this is

like saying, $5 + 5 = 0$, with a carry, in the decimal system)

ADD = half-add (XOR) plus carry (AND)

Similarly, for subtraction

-		half-add	borrow	
0	0	0	0	$0 - 0 = 0$
0	1	1	1	$0 - 1 = 0$, with a borrow
1	0	1	0	$1 - 0 = 0$
1	1	0	0	$1 - 1 = 0$

SUB = half-add (XOR) plus borrow (one of the unnamed functions)

We can see that mathematics in the binary system can be implemented with logical functions.

X (times)			multiply
0	0	0	0 x 0 = 0
0	1	0	0 x 1 = 0
1	0	0	1 x 0 = 0
1	1	1	1 x 1 = 1

Multiplication is the AND function.

Division

/			
0	0	not allowed	0/0 = not allowed
0	1	0	0/1 = 0
1	0	not allowed	1/0 = not allowed
1	1	1	1/1 = 1

Division is another of the unnamed operations.

An important issue in computing is the choice of a base for the number system. We do base 10 because we have 10 fingers. Digital computers, with on/off switching elements, do base 2 mathematics. Actually, any base will work. We like to use base-10, but we could as easily use binary on our 10 fingers to represent quantities up to 1023 (without taking off our shoes). Our current microelectronics technology supports base 2. Mechanical calculators and computers can support base 10.

Symbols in the binary system are 0 and 1.These can be represented by on/off, +12/-12 volts, n-magnetic/s-magnetic, whatever physical phenomenon has two states.

A byte is a collection of 8 bits. This makes for a handy size. In binary, a byte can represent 1 of 256 (2^8) possible states or values.

A computer word is a collection of 8, 16, 24, 13, 97, or some other number of bits. The number of bits collected into a word does not need to be a power of two. The range of numbers we can represent depends on how many bits we have in the word. This determines the complexity of the implementation.

Binary Coded Decimal uses 10 of the possible 16 codes in 4 bits. The other bit patterns are not used, or could be used to indicate sign, error, overflow, or such. BCD converts to decimal easily, and provides a precise representation of decimal numbers. It requires serial by digit calculations, but gives exact results. It uses more storage than binary integers, and the implementation of the logic for operations is a bit more complex. It is an alternative to the limited range or precision of binary integers, and the complexity of floating point. BCD is used extensively in instrumentation and personal calculators. Support for operations on BCD numbers were provided in the IBM mainframes, and the Intel x86 series of microprocessors.

BCD 4 bit code, only 10 valid values:

0000 = 0 0001 = 1 0010 = 2 0011 = 3 0100 = 4
0101 = 5 0110 = 6 0111 = 7 1000 = 8 1001 = 9

1010, 1011, 1100, 1101, 1110, 1111 are invalid number codes in BCD.

Arithmetic operations in BCD format numbers are usually done in binary, and then adjusted to handle the carry (or borrow). For example, in packed BCD, we may generate a carry between the 3rd and 4th bit position. Subtraction is usually implemented by adding the 10's complement of the subtrahend. The 10's complement is formed by taking the 9's complement, and then adding one. The 9's complement can be formed by subtracting the digits from 9. If a BCD arithmetic operation generates an invalid BCD result, 6 can be added to force a carry. BCD strings of numbers can have a "decimal point" inserted wherever convenient. Additional bookkeeping is then needed to keep the numbers commensurate for addition and subtraction, and to adjust in multiplication and division.

An 8-bit processor can operate with 8-bit data, which can represent the unsigned integers from 0 to 255 decimal. If we need to represent the algebraic sign, we need to give up on bit, to represent -128 to plus 127, 0 being considered a positive number. The normal method of representing negative numbers is the 2's complement scheme.

There are many ways to do represent negative numbers. The case we are familiar with from our use of decimal is the use of a special symbol "-". This gives us the sign-magnitude format.

We could do this in binary as well, and, in addition, there are the 1's complement and 2's complement schemes of representing negative numbers. To form the 1's complement of a binary number, change all bits to their logical complement. Problem is, in a finite (closed) number system, the 1's complement system gives two different representations of zero (i.e., +0 and -0), both valid. To form the 2's complement, do the 1's complement and add 1. This is a more complex operation, but the advantage is, there is only one representation of zero. Because zero is considered a positive number, there is one more negative number than positive number in this representation. Two's complement has become the dominant choice for negative number representation in computers.

One's complement was used on the Univac 1108 series mainframes. A problem was that 0 and -0 did not test equal. That can be a problem. The equivalent to the complements in the decimal system is 9's complement and 10's complement, but these are not taught any more, and don't get used much.

Subtraction

Subtraction can be accomplished by addition of the complement. We don't need a separate subtracter circuit. We can use the adder, and we need a complement (inverter) circuit, which is easy. Logical operations such as complement operate on a bit-by-bit basis with no "carry" or "borrow" from adjacent bits, like we would find in mathematical operations.

Subtraction example

-	0	1	b	0	1
	b=borrow				
0	0	1	0	0	0
1	1	0	1	1	0

Remember a-b does not equal b-a. Subtraction depends on the order of the operands.

If division is equivalent to repeated subtraction, and subtraction is the same as the addition of the complement, and multiplication is repeated addition, then all we really need is an addition circuit, and a complementer. Since addition can be accomplished by the logic circuits AND and XOR, we can in theory implement all binary mathematical operations in terms of logic functions. That's the theory. It works. There's better ways to do it.

Multiplication

Multiplication by digit is possible, but can take excessive time, with long digits. The multiplication table in binary is rather simple, though. Only one of the four cases results in a non-zero result. The multiplication of two n-bit numbers requires n^2 operations. The results for a multiplication of two n-bit numbers can be 2n bits wide.

Shift-and-add is a common multiplication technique in binary. Shifting gives us successive powers of two. There do exist special algorithms for multiplication and division, so we don't need to do repeated adds or subtracts. We can also design a digital multiplier for hexadecimal numbers, so we do 4 binary digits per clock. This can make use of a look-up table.

Multiplication of fractions takes the form of normal multiplication, with due diligence of the resulting binary point.

In optimizing integer multiplications, we can speed up the process where we have a variable multiplied by a constant. First, if the constant is a power of two, the multiplication can be accomplished with shifts. Similarly, multiplication by sums of powers of two is also easily handled (i.e., 6 = 4+2, 10 = 8+2). With a bit more work, we can factor the fixed multiplicand into powers of two (i.e., 13 = 8 + 4 + 1; 15 = 16 - 1) and accomplish the multiplication with shifts and adds. This works for fairly complex numbers, because the cost of a multiply instruction is high, whereas the shifts, adds, and subtracts are usually optimized to be single clock operations. This technique requires knowledge of the individual instruction times.

Division is a big, ugly, and time-consuming operation, to be avoided whenever possible. The division operation is usually the slowest one in the instruction set. This sets a lower limit to interrupt latency in real-time systems, and can certainly effect system throughput.

A special case, of division is the reciprocal, 1/X. Here, the numerator of the fraction is known, and the division easier. After forming the reciprocal, which takes less time than an arbitrary division, a multiplication is required.

$$A/B = A \times (1/B)$$

In integer multiplication, division of a value by a power of two can be accomplished by shifts.

For 8-bit multiply, we could calculate all of the possible 256 answers, and store them in a ROM, then look up the answer using one of the parameters as an index. Note that an 8x8 multiply results in a 16 bit answer, so we would need 256 bytes x 2 of storage, or 512 bytes. This was a lot of memory at the time, and resulted in a classic time versus memory versus money trade-off. Multiplication of BCD digits was easier, as there were only 10x10, or 100 cases.

16 bit math on an 8-bit machine.

If we needed to do 16-bit math on signed, 8-bit integers on an 8-bit machine, it was possible, but slower. For an ADD operation, we would add the two lower two bytes, and ADC, add with previous carry in, the high two bytes. Similarly with the Subtract and Subtract with borrow. This could be extended to 24, 32, or even 64 bits, but it was a slow process. And, in the original 8080, the borrow bit was not set correctly by the hardware.

If we needed to do a 16x16 multiply on an 8 bit machine, we could implement this as a loop, with one parameter being added to itself, using the other input as the loop counter. We could also use a process with partial products being calculated and added. This was also a slow operation. It was important to check for overflow as well, since the result required 32 bits. Beyond 16 bits, this could really be complicated. We could also consider the table look up approach, but now the ROM size was prohibitively large.

Division of a 16-bit entity by an 8-bit, or 16 bits divided by 16 bits can be accomplished in a subtraction loop. Here, it is important to check for sign change, which requires the loop be backed up one step, and a remainder stored.

Why do calculators seem to do multiplication and division so fast? They are faster than you, but not really

fast. Ask an HP calculator to do 99! (factorial = 1*2*3…
*n) and watch the display blank for a while, while its
thinking.

The 16-bit arc-hyperbolic-cotangent calculation on an 8-
bit machine with no multiply or divide instruction is left
as an exercise for the student. Do let me know.

Basis Technology, Logic families

Computer architectures can be implemented in different
basis technologies. Charles Babbage implemented his
decimal-based different engines in mechanical
technology in the 1840's. Vacuum tubes were the basis
of World War-II mainframes. This lead to discrete
transistors, and then to integrated circuits, using multiple
transistors in a package. These building blocks were
organized as specific logic gates. There are a number of
different basis sets of logic gates to be able to implement
the common logic functions (negate, AND, OR, XOR).
The laws of Boolean Algebra allow for deriving different
functions from these. We will focus here on the
electrical, integrated circuit technology's to implement
the logical designs.

RTL or resistor-transistor logic was derived from the
early vacuum tube technology and discrete components.
It was the basis of many early mainframe computers, as
an evolution from relay implementations. RTL logic
chips were developed by Fairchild Semiconductor for the
Apollo Guidance Computer in 1962. Diode-transistor

logic was developed by Signetics, Westinghouse, and Fairchild. It was used in the 1962 Minuteman-II missile guidance computer. Motorola's ECL, emitter coupled logic, was a high power, high speed logic implementation.

Sylvania introduced transistor-transistor logic (TTL) in 1963. This was quickly followed by a family of devices from Texas Instruments. The switching elements are transistors.

Metal oxide semiconductor refers to the manufacture of a semiconductor device with a metal layer and an oxide insulating layer. This can be done with an n-type semiconductor material (electrons predominate) or a p-type material (lack of electrons ("holes") predominate). The NMOS technology has a faster switching time. The next technique used a combination of n-type and p-type call CMOS, or complementary metal oxide semiconductor. The breakthrough achieved was that CMOS technology only consumes power when changing state. Very little power is used in a given logic state, as compared to previous technologies. CMOS can also operate with lower voltages, leading to further reductions in power. Power leads to heat, which limits the number of switches in a package.

A special purpose hardware device, purpose-built, will always be faster than a general purpose device programmed or configured for a specific task. This means that purpose-built hardware is the best, yet least flexible choice. Programmability provides flexibility, and reduces the cost of change. A new approach, provided by *FPGA* technology, gives us the ability to reconfigure the hardware and well as the software. This is applicable even to 8-bit processors, as they are available and can be implemented in the FPGA. This can be to replace legacy implementations. In many applications, 8 bits is enough.

Monolithic microprocessor

The microprocessors started out as multi-chip units, because all of the functionality would not fit on a single chip, given the technology of the time. As the technology advanced the processor became a single-chip, monolithic unit. Further down the technology road, memory and I/O functions could be implemented on the chip as well. Consider the IBM pc. The initial motherboard contained about 200 integrated packages. Current pc motherboards contain the 64-bit CPU, two custom chips (the "northbridge" and the "southbridge"), and a few cache memory chips.

The ALU

An arithmetic logic unit (ALU) performs arithmetic (add, subtract, compare) and logical operations (AND, OR, XOR, negate) on data. The concept was developed by John von Neumann in 1945, in the development of the EDVAC computer. An example of an ALU is the Texas Instruments 74181, the first complete ALU on a chip. Earlier CPU's required a large circuit board of 100's discrete logic chips, or even multiple boards. The 74181 contains 75 logic gates, and is a 4-bit wide CPU, that can be used in multiple units to expand the ALU to 8, 12, or 16 bits wide. It implements 16 mathematical and 16 logical operations on 4-bit data in 22 nanoseconds. Later units implemented in a different technology could accomplish these in 7 nanoseconds. Multiply and divide operations can be synthesized by multiple steps in the control unit. Multiply is implemented with repeated ADD's, and divide by repeated subtracts. Shifts can also be synthesized in the firmware. Computer designs using the 74181 included the Data General NOVA 16-bit minicomputer, circa 1968, the DEC PDP-11, the Xerox Alto, the first computer to have a GUI, and the 32-bit DEC Vax-11/780. An example of an 8-bit ALU is the Texas instruments 74AS888 chip. The Motorola MC14581CL was the first CMOS ALU.

The Control Unit

The Control Unit decodes the instructions as they are read from memory, and tells each functional unit of the ALU what to do at each clock cycle. It can be implemented as a state machine. The control unit instantiates the instruction set architecture of the computer. The control unit can be hard-wired to decode each instruction, or it can do this task by table look-up in memory. The hard-wired approach is the fastest, but the look-up alternative provides a flexibility to modify and extend the instruction set, within the limitations of the fixed hardware. The definition of the instructions is contained in a read-only memory as firmware. Some write-able memory can be provided to add new instructions. This technique originated in mainframe computers. As the technology advanced, it became possible to include the control unit on the same silicon as the ALU.

Bit slice

The bit slice approach allows you to use modular units to build a CPU as wide as you need. The usual building block size is 4 bits wide, and you can use, for example, 4 of these to implement a 16-bit machine. The control logic is common to all 4 of the ALU chips. Carry's and borrows must propagate along the ALU of course. Besides the 74181 previously discussed, bit slice units included the AMD Am2900, the National Semiconductor IMP-8, and the Intel 3000. The technique was used in the 1956 EDSAC-2 machine, by the University of Cambridge.

The IMP-00A was introduced by National in 1973. It used PMOS technology, and was clocked at 700 KHz. It became the basis of the IMP-8 CPU. National referred to the base 4-bit device as a RALU, 7 registers and the arithmetic/logic unit. It had an associated control read-only memory, the CROM, which could hold 100 instructions. These came preprogrammed with a 4-bit, 8-bit, or a 16-bit standard instruction set.

Photos courtesy, cpushack.com

The Intel 3000 was a bipolar (TTL) bit slice machine in widths of 2 bits. The 3001 was the control unit, and the 3002 was the arithmetic unit. The 3002 operated with a 6

MHz clock, and had 512 microinstructions. There were eleven general purpose registers. The 3001 control unit had a 512 word microprogram ROM, and could also address external ROM. It also controlled the carry-in/carry-out for the arithmetic logic units. The 3001 was a 2's complement, 2-bit wide ALU. It included a set of 11 scratchpad registers, and an accumulator. The chip implemented addition, subtraction, the logic functions. The 3214 provided priority interrupt support, the 3003 added look-ahead carry functionality. The CPU was second-sourced by Signetics.

AMD 2901

The AMD 2901 was a 4-bit slice machine. It included the ALU and 16 registers. The 2910 was the control processor. The 2903 was a later ALU with hardware multiply.

Western Digital also produced a bit slice machine. The ALU was 8-bits wide and had 26 registers. The control unit operated with microcode ROMS. Standard ROM sets were available for the DEC LSI-11 and a Pascal micro-engine.

Associated memory chips

Generally, the density of memory chips followed the same exponential growth curve ("Moore's Law") as the processors they supported. Memory is a much simpler device, highly regular. The 8-bit CPU manufacturers almost all started out making silicon memory to replace the older magnetic core, and later branched out in processors.

RAM

In RAM, random access memory, any element accessible in the same clock time, as opposed to sequential media, such a tape or a disk. In *sequential media*, the access time varies, and depends on the order of access. This is true for disks or drums, where the item requested probably just went by the read heads, and another rotation of the platter is required. Of course, mechanical systems, in operation, tend to wear out faster because of their moving parts.

A memory can be considered as a black-box with two functions, read and write. With the write function, we present the memory with two inputs: the data item, and an address. There is no output. The memory associated the data item with the address and remembers it. On the read function, we present the memory with the address, and expect to get back the data item previously associated with it.

Other design choices in memory include volatility. The memory may forget after a period of time. That's not good. Although, depending on the timing, the data can be read out and written back just in time. This is the basis for dynamic memory. Is there such a thing as totally non-volatile memory? One of the earliest memory types, magnetic core, was persistent when the power was turned off. It is unclear how long the data was retained. It is speculated that the original code for the Saturn Launch Vehicle is still resident in the core in the flight computers of the Saturn's on display.

Volatile memory includes static semiconductor RAM and dynamic RAM. Static RAM uses a flip-flop, and retains its contents as long as the power remains. Static RAM is faster, less dense, and consumes more power than dynamic RAM. Dynamic RAM is more dense, usually by a power of 4, due to a simpler structure, but requires refresh. It forgets in fractions of a second, because the information is stored as a charge on a capacitor, which leaks away. Why would anyone use this as a storage media? It is cheap, easily mass produced, the "forget" time is eons to a computer chip, and the overhead of the refresh operation is minimal. A separate chip, or the CPU usually does the refresh, because the memory is not usable during that time. The memory can be organized into sections, so a refresh in one section still allows access in others.

Non-volatile memory includes various types of read-only memory, and battery-backed static RAM which has a life of several years, depending on the battery source.

Even read-only memory is written at least at once. Actually, a ROM (read-only memory) is manufactured with a specific pattern of 1's and 0's built in. For prototyping, various types of programmable read-only memory are used. These can be written and erased multiple times. Earlier, ultraviolet light was used to erase the devices to an all-1's state. These chips had glass windows. Later, the contents became reprogrammable or alterable with higher voltage levels, and could be modified in-circuit. Both the ultraviolet-erasable versions (UV-PROM's) and the Electrically alterable forms (EEPROMs) tended to forget over time. Before this phenomenon was understood, these types of parts were included in deployed systems, that failed during later use.

Memory organization

Semiconductor Memory, like all current microelectronics, is a 2-dimensional structure. Thus, density usually goes up by a factor of four, as we double the width and the height. Memory is a very regular structure, amenable to mass production. In random access memory we address bytes, or words. In the 8-bit processor the word is a byte. Generally, memory is accessed in parallel bytes. The initial memory chips were 1 bit wide, and arranged in groups of 8. As the technology advanced, the chips got greater capacity.

Associated Support and I/O chips

Specialized chips for support functions to the CPU evolved along with the CPU and memory. These would handle, for example, interrupts, direct memory access, dynamic memory refresh, and such tasks. These will be discussed in the sections with the CPU's.

Clock generator

The CPU and the control unit require a clock to synchronize their operations. This is derived from a crystal oscillator. The early 8-bit CPU's required complex, multi-phase clocks. This evolved into simpler single phase clocks. As PMOS and NMOS technology gave way to CMOS, it was possible to implement variable rate clocks, and the designs allowed for stopping the clock without a loss of state in the CPU. CMOS technology power dissipation goes up or down linearly as with the clock rate.

Microcontroller

A microcontroller is a simple CPU plus some memory and Input-output. The idea is to have a single-chip solution to minimize costs. Microcontrollers are not used as general number crunchers, but in dedicated control applications such as elevators, gas pumps, and cell phones. The controller can have both RAM and ROM memory, for data and code. It can usually also access external memory to expand either or both, although the goal with a microcontroller is a single-chip system.

With ROM memory, the part is manufactured with the customer code built-in, and it is an expensive and costly process to change it. Special versions of the microcontroller with EPROM are usually available for prototyping, allowing for commitment to a manufactured part only when the code has been verified.

1-bit Processor

The MC14500B Industrial Control Unit from Motorola is a 1-bit processor for very simple control applications. It can implement the old relay-based ladder logic. It did not have a program counter. It operated at 100 KHz, and had 16 instructions. It has been used in HVAC systems and other simple control applications. It is implemented in a 16-pin package. The instructions include the logical operations on the single bit data type, as well as load and store. There is a conditional skip instruction. The 14500 clocks an external program counter for memory access to 4-bit op codes.

2-bit processor

The Intel 3002 was a bit slice CPU of width 2. The 3000 series was discussed in the previous bit slice section of this document.

4-bit Processors

Before the 8-bit processors came the 4-bit processors. Actually, 4-bits makes sense – it can handle the binary coded decimal (BDC) numbers, 10 digits contained in a 4-bit word, with 6 symbols left over. For calculator use, BCD representation works fine, and serial-by-digit calculation fast enough. Both Texas Instruments and Hewlett Packard developed calculator chips using BCD math. Although 4-bit general purpose CPU's were developed first, these quickly evolved into 8-bit architectures. But, 4-bit microcontrollers are still being used today, mostly where extremely low power is required, and computation demands are not high. Generally, a 4-bit processor operates on 4-bit wide data, and has 8-bit wide addresses.

Intel 4004 and 4040

Early examples of the 4-bit processors were the Intel 4004 and 4040. The 4004 is generally considered the world's first commercially available microprocessor. The general-purpose 18-pin chip, the 4004, in November 1971. It incorporated both the ALU and the control unit. It had a clock speed of 740 KHz,used 2,300 transistors, and was produced on 2" diameter wafers with a 10-micrometer line width. The instruction cycle required 8 clock cycles, or 10.8 microseconds. It had ports for ROM, RAM, and I/O, and was originally designed for use in a calculator. There were 16 general purpose 4-bit registers. Its instruction set architecture had been inspired by the DEC PDP-8. It included 46 instructions. Interestingly, the little 4004 chip had at least the same processor power of the circa 1946 Eniac computer, which out-weighted it by 33 tons. The clock rate was 500 KHz, later raised to 740 KHz. Associated support chips included the 4001 ROM, the 4002 RAM, the 4003 shift unit, and 4008 and 09 EPROM interface chips. The chip operated from a single 14 volt supply. To interface with TTL logic, two supplies of +5 and -9 were used.

Photo courtesy cpushack.com

The later 4040 model brought logical and compare instructions to the 4004 architecture, with an instruction count of 60. The 4040 used 3,000 transistors, and had a larger stack, a larger program space, and more registers than the 4004.

Photo courtesy cpushack.com.

Nippon Calculating Machinery Company approached Intel about producing 12 custom chips for their Busicom 141 printing calculator. Intel suggested a 4 chip set: CPU, RAM, ROM, and I/O. This was produced as the 4004. It was capable of a blazing 60,000 operations per second. It was too slow for the calculator application, so Intel later bought back the rights to it. They had a true stored program, general purpose computer in a chip. The rest is history.

Support chips for the 4040 included:

4201 – Clock Generator 500 to 740 KHz using 4 to 5.185 MHz crystals
4308 – 1 KB ROM
4207 – 8-bit output port
4209 – 8-bit input port
4211 – 8-bit I/O port
4289 – Standard Memory Interface
4702 – 256 byte UVPROM
4316 – 2 KB ROM
4101 – 256 x 4-bit word RAM

Photo courtesy cpushack.com.

The 4004 was used on the Pioneer-10 Deep Space Mission, launched in 1972. The mission studied the asteroid belt, the solar wind, Jupiter, and the outer reaches of the solar system. The computer was used to hold, decode, and distribute commands transmitted from Earth. The mission lasted until 2003, when communications was lost due to distance, a duration of 30 years. As of March 2011, the spacecraft is some 102

Astronomical Units (AU= 93 million miles) from the Sun, and radio (or sunlight) takes 14 hours to get to and from it.

A modern 4-bit processor can be found in an appliance controller role, and is frequently used in microwave ovens. 4-bits is sufficient. The DMC42C3008 has a 4-bit ALU, 8 kbytes of ROM, 512 nibbles of RAM, and integral I/O devices such as timer/counters, an 8-bit A/D converter, an interval and a watchdog timer, a PWM, and serial communication. It includes its clock oscillator.

I/O is memory mapped, and there are 4 registers as well as an accumulator. There are 4 external vectored interrupts, and 6 internal interrupt sources.

The Apollo-Soyuz (joint US-Russian manned mission, circa 1975) flew with a Hewlett-Packard model HP-65 scientific calculator, used to calculate critical course-correction maneuvers. The HP calculators used a proprietary 4-bit binary coded decimal (BCD) chip, and serial-by-digit calculations.

TMS-1000

According to the Smithsonian Institution, Texas Instruments engineers Gary Boone and Michael Cochran created the first microcontroller and the first single chip CPU in 1971. The result of their work was the TMS-1000, which went commercial in 1974. It was widely used in embedded applications such as toys (the TI

Speak-n-Spell), games, appliances, burglar alarms, copy machines, and more. It was used in TI calculators, starting with the TI-16, and including the TI-35. There was a family of TMS-1000 parts with different configurations

TI filed for a patent, and Gary Boone was awarded U.S. Patent 3,757,306 for the single-chip microprocessor architecture on September 4, 1973. We may never know which company actually had the first working microprocessor running on the lab bench. In 1971 and again in 1976, Intel and TI entered into broad patent cross-licensing agreements, with Intel paying royalties to TI for the microprocessor patent. A history of these events is contained in court documentation from a legal dispute between Cyrix and Intel, with TI as intervener and owner of the microprocessor patent.

A computer-on-a-chip combines the microprocessor core (CPU), memory, and I/O (input/output) lines onto one chip. The computer-on-a-chip patent, called the "microcomputer patent" at the time, U.S. Patent 4,074,351, was awarded to Gary Boone and Michael J. Cochran of TI. Aside from this patent, the standard meaning of microcomputer is a computer using one or more microprocessors as its CPU(s), while the concept defined in the patent is more akin to what is now called a microcontroller.

The PMOS, 300 KHz, TMS-1000 had 8192 bits of ROM, 256 bits of RAM, and a 4-bit ALU in a single package. There was a 4-bit input port, and 19 outputs. The instruction decoder is programmable, so the instruction set is not rigidly defined. There are 43 standard instructions, with the ability to add more via microinstructions. Later versions featured more RAM and ROM, and CMOS versions were available. The PMOS versions operated at 15 volts.

Rockwell PPS-4

The PPS-4 CPU was developed for calculator use. It operated at 200 KHz and used a PMOS technology. It became available in 1972. Some units were used as microcontrollers in pinball machines. The early versions were made by Rockwell.

Atmel MARC4

The Marc4 is a 4-bit FORTH microcontroller. It is a Harvard stack-based architecture, with 256 4-bit words of RAM and 9 Kbytes of ROM, with eight vectored interrupts, and a software interrupt. More than 4096 words of memory can be accessed by the 12-bit wide program counter, and memory banking. There are six general purpose registers, and one condition code register. Because of the use of the Forth stack-based language, the MARC-4 is a zero-address machine since the operands reside on the stack.

HP Saturn

The HP Saturn microprocessors were used in their line of programmable calculators. The first unit was the HP-71B in 1984. The processors used 4-bit BCD representation data. The internal 4 general purpose and 5 scratch data registers are 64 bits wide. Addressing is via 20 bits, for 1 million, 4-bit entities.

NEC µPD75X

NEC Electronics (now Renesas Corp, Tokyo) µPD612xA, µPD613x, µPD6x, and µPD1724 are 4-bit infrared remote control transmitter microcontrollers.

EM Microelectronics EM6600 family

These are ultra-lower power microcontrollers available in 8-pin packages, and frequently used for power control. The EM 6882r includes a 4-bit ADC, watchdog timer, PWM, and a 10-bit up/down counter. There are 80 words of 4-bit RAM, and 1536 words of 16-bit ROM. The CPU is RISC architecture, with 2 clock cycles per instruction. There are 72 instructions. Included is an 8-bit serial interface. There are 2 external interrupts.

Epson S1C63 family

These are high-end 4–bit CMOS MCU's with a variety of rom, ram, and I/O features. The core CPU can address 64k 13-bit data words. The instruction set has 47 types with 5 different addressing modes, and there are a series of registers. Most instructions take one cycle. The chip has a 2-stage pipeline. It supports 15 vectored interrupts, and has a software interrupt, as well as an NMI.

Others

Other 4-bit processors included the Fairchild Camera & Instrument PPS-25. This was a 1972 multichip model, operating at 400 MHz, in PMOS technology. A variation of this was used in a calculator chipset. The NEC uCom4 operated at 1 MHz, and used 2500 transistors in NMOS technology. The National IMP-4 operated at 500 KHz, and was a multichip arrangement in PMOS. Also-rans included the Microsystem MC-1 and theToshiba TLCS-47 series.

The author found a modern 4-bit microcontroller lurking in his old microwave oven when he disassembled it to see why it had failed. The Daewoo DMC423008 model is a CMOS 4-bit processor with 8kbytes of ROM and 512 4-bit data words of RAM. Program memory is 10 bits wide. There are eight 4-bit registers, vectored interrupts (4 external, 6 internal), a watchdog timer, an interval timer, an 8-bit counter, PWM, 8-bit serial port, an 8-bit A/D converter, and 31 I/O pins. But, it looked like the magnetron tube shorted out, negating the effects of the microcontroller.

8-bit processors

Eight bit processors operate on 8-bit wide data, and generally have a 16 bit address. They need support chips such as memory and I/O devices. The microcontrollers, as opposed to the CPU's, include memory and I/O on the same chip. They are designed to be stand-alone, for minimal chip count embedded applications.

The Intel 8008

The 8008 was the first 8-bit monolithic microprocessor to market. It was originally designed for Intel's customer Control Terminal Corp, in their Datapoint 2200, whose design existed as TTL logic chips on a board. Work was begun on the 8008 before the 4004, but the 8008 didn't go into production in April of 1972. The advantage of 8-bits over 4 was not more calculating ability, but the need to handle 8-bit ASCII characters.

It operated up to 800 MHz, had 3,500 transistors in a PMOS technology, with 10 micron line width. There were 48 instructions. The address space was 16 kilobytes, but direct addressing was not supported. The H and L registers had to be loaded with the memory address. The 8008 required a complex clock, and significant amounts of external logic. It was eventually second-sourced by Microsystems International and Siemens.

Intel 8080

The 8080 was a great improvement over the prior 8008 chip, incorporating many features into the chip that required the use of external hardware with the 8008. It could be considered a superset of thr 8008 design. The 8080 was an NMOS design, with 8-bit words and a 16-bit address bus. It required plus and minus 5 volts and plus 12 volts. It drew 0.8 watts. The circa-1973 chip was a sequential state machine design, where the current state is a function of the previous state, and current inputs. It used 6,000 transistors, and operated at 2 MHz (later, 3 MHz). It was designed by Federico Faggin, and released in 1974. It had 48 instructions.

There were four control inputs: READY, which was a wait state request, and could be held indefinitely; HOLD, which was a DMA request; INT, which was the interrupt request; and RESET, which initialized the processor by clearing the Program Counter and Interrupt Request registers, the INTR and HLDA states. The HALT is cleared, and execution begins when the RESET is removed. Control inputs were asynchronous with the processors internal clock. Instructions took one to five machine cycles, depending on memory access. There were eleven types of machine cycles, taking 3, 4, or 5 machine states. A machine state was marked by successive phase 1 clocks. Machine cycles could include instruction fetch, memory read or write, I/O read or write, stack read or write, interrupt acknowledge and halt, interrupt acknowledge while halted, and null. At reset, the 8080 started execution at location zero.

The interrupt sequence for the 8080 started when the external device asserted the INTR line. When the CPU finished the currently executing instruction, and assuming interrupts were not disabled in software, it responds with the IORQ signal. At this point, the interrupting device is expected to provide a valid 8080 instruction on the data lines. Although there are many amusing things that could happen at this point, it was best if the interrupting device supplied the one-byte RST instruction. This was an autovector to 1 of 8 predefined locations in memory – essentially a vectored interrupt process.

The 8080 used a two-phase, non-overlapping clock. Typical cycle time was a microsecond. The phases were referred to as PHI-1 and PHI-2. State was determined by successive PHI-1 clocks. This was the minimal unit of processing activity. A machine cycle was 3, 4, or 5 states.

There were six timing and control outputs. The SYNC signal said that the processor status was placed on the data bus. This could then be latched externally by SYNC and-ed with clock signal PHI-1. DBIN, or data bus in, showed the bi-directional data bus was in input mode.

WAIT indicated that the processor was in wait state. /WR indicated that the data bus was in write mode, and there was output on the data bus. HLDA was the hold acknowledge. The data and address busses were tri-stated at this point. INTE showed whether the CPU would respond to interrupts. With 16 address lines, the processor could address 64k bytes of memory. The program counter and stack pointers were both 16 bits. The Program Counter held the next memory location to be fetched and executed. For the stack, a PUSH operation resulted in a decrement, and a POP operation resulted in the SP being incremented. The stack is just a first-in, first-out data structure implemented in random access memory. It is sometimes referred to as a zero-address memory, because all the action happens implicitly where the stack pointer points. There is a stack status signal that allows for a separate stack memory pace for security reasons. But, the stack resides in RAM.

There were six general-purpose 8-bit registers (B, C, D, E, H, L) that could be used as three 16 bit register pairs (B-C, D-E, H-L). The accumulator was 8 bits wide, and had five associated flags. These flag bits indicated the results of the previous operation: Zero, Carry, Sign, Parity, and Auxiliary Carry. The Arithmetic Logic Unit (ALU) could do arithmetic, logical, and rotate operations on data.

The instruction cycle is the time to fetch and execute an instruction. Depending on the number of memory accesses required, the instruction cycle was 1-5 machine cycles. The instruction fetch was one cycle, and up to four memory accesses might be required for data.

There were eleven different types of machine cycles in the 8080: Instruction fetch, or the M1 cycle, Memory (non-instruction) Read, Memory Write, I/O Read, I/O Write, Stack Read and Write, Interrupt Acknowledge, Halt Acknowledge, Interrupt Acknowledge while halted, and NULL, which was used during interrupt processing. During this state, the program counter was not incremented, the memory read signal was not generated, and an instruction was fetched from the interrupting device. More about this when we discuss interrupts.

How do we get out of a HALT state? We got in by executing a HALT instruction. We need to assert the RESET signal, the HOLD (which, when released, gets us back to HALT), and then Interrupt. Notice that HALT when interrupts are disabled is fatal. One can only turn the power off and back on again. A later invention was the non-maskable interrupt.

Interrupts enhance I/O response time, by allowing external events to interrupt the processing flow of the CPU. Like when the phone rings while I'm typing this. Sometimes you don't want to allow interrupts for a period of time, because there is a critical task to be done. A CPU can mask them off. I can turn off the phone.

In the 8080, when an interrupt occurs, the interrupting device supplies the next instruction. It better be a good one. A one byte instruction is easiest, but multi-byte instructions are possible. The Restart instruction is a good choice, because it is a one-byte subroutine call (or vector).

There are eight Restart instructions, numbered 0 to 7. They automatically go to addresses starting at 0 and incrementing by 8; Restart 7 goes to 38H. In this scheme, the interrupting device can supply one of the Restart instructions, which will jump to a fixed predetermined location, and execute the code there. We only have 8 bytes, so we probably put a JUMP instruction there. This is the concept of a vectored interrupt, using a table of vectored addresses. The Interrupt Service routine, the piece of code that does what we interrupted the flow of the processor to do, can be anywhere in memory, pointed to by the JUMP instruction we put in the fixed location table. But, two cautions: The table of addresses in memory must have proper contents before an interrupt occurs, and the proper code must reside at the target address. This is part of the initialization process. The state machine doesn't care if we load something there or not – it will use the contents of memory as the instruction to be executed, and, as Von Neumann allows, we execute data (or stack contents).

One common problem was to only load the interrupt vectors that were being used. Then, invariably, a "rogue" interrupt caused by noise would vector through the non-initialized memory to a random location, and begin executing data, causing vast resources to be expended upon debugging (and many bad words to be said).

The Intel approach to Input-Output is to use a separate I/O address space and I/O instructions. This does not preclude using memory-mapped I/O. The 8080 had 256 inputs and 256 outputs, each one byte wide. (Thus, the I/O address was 8 bits). The Accumulator register held the I/O address.

Once the 8080 was accepted by the microcomputer community, other variations of the hardware appeared by Intel and their competitors. The 9080 was AMD's version of the 8080, with a correction made to an oversight in the Intel design regarding the auxiliary carry bit during subtraction. There were some licensing and intellectual property issues with Intel, and AMD discontinued the part after obtaining the manufacturing license for the 8080 from Intel. Intel later made a companion chip to the 8080, the 8231, for hardware multiply.

The 8080 was second-sourced by AMD, Mitsubishi, NEC, National Semiconductor, and Texas Instruments.

Floating Point

In 1975, the Lawrence Livermore Laboratory of the University of California published the source code for an 8008/8080 floating point software package. This implemented add, subtract, multiply, divide, and square root. This package used a 24-bit signed mantissa, and a 6-bit signed exponent. Format conversion was supported.

In the 1970's, Intel and AMD made two cross-licensed models of floating-point processor chips.

The floating point format adds dynamic range to calculations, in trade for absolute accuracy. The standard ALU operated on binary integer data. A floating point number has two parts, a mantissa, and an exponent. Floating point is much like scientific or engineering notation.

The Intel 8231 and 8231A were non-IEEE floating point format chips that supported sine, cosine, tangent, etc. The IEEE Standard for floating point computation and format had not yet been established. The later Intel 8232 did support IEEE floating point but not sine, cosine, tan, and the other transcendental functions.

Images courtesy cpushack.com

The AMD 9511 and 9511A were compatible with the Intel 8231. The later AMD 9512 was compatible with Intel 8232, and supported IEEE floating point.

Images courtesy cpushack.com

The 8231 was termed an arithmetic processing unit, and the 8232 was called a floating point unit. Both could convert fixed to floating, and vice versa. Intel was heavily involved with the development of the IEEE Floating Point Standard at the time.

These were designed for use with 8080 or similar processors and used an 8-bit data bus. They were interfaced to a host system either through programmed I/O or a DMA controller. There use was not restricted to the Intel architecture family chips. The chips were developed by AMD, and licensed to Intel in exchange for the rights to their 8080 and 8085.

These chips used a simple protocol to accept data and floating point instructions, to produce a result. They were intended to supplement a microprocessor and accessed as an I/O device. The chips ran from a 1MHz clock, later 2MHz. At the cost of time, these chips added a tremendous processing capability to the 8-bit units. A floating point add would take some 54-368 clock cycles. A multiply could take up to 168 cycles. X^y could take up to 12,000 cycles. Transcendental functions were calculated with polynomial approximations.

The 8080 chip found use about a variety of space missions, including NASA's OSS-1, 2, and 3 Shuttle-attached pallets, Hubble Space Telescope, International Sun-Earth Explorer, Seasat, and the French Meteosat program and OTS missions. The OSS attached pallets onboard the Space Shuttle were not exposed to the harsh environment of space for extended periods.

Intel 8085

The 8085 was an advanced version of the 8080. It had two new instructions to enable/disable three added interrupt pins (and the serial I/O pins). It also featured simplified hardware that required only a single +5V supply, and included a clock-generator and bus-controller circuits on the chip. It was binary compatible with the 8080, but required less supporting hardware, allowing simpler and less expensive microcomputer systems to be built. It went into production in April of 1976.

The 8085 incorporated the features of several support chips for the 8080, including the 8224 clock generator and the 8228 system controller. The 8085 just needed the 8156 ROM and 8355 or 8755 ROM/PROM. The 8085 used a multiplexed data/address bus to reduce chip pin-out. This required external de-multiplexing of the 16-bit address and the 8-bit data. The chip operated to 6 MHZ eventually. There were 48 instructions. It supported vectored interrupts. Intel produced a hardware multiply/divide chip called the 8231 to augment the 8085. The popular 8085 was second sourced by AMD, National, Mitsubishi, Toshiba, NEC, and Siemens.

Support chips included the 8155, a 3k static RAM with I/O ports and timer, the 8355, a 16k ROM and I/O, the 8755, a 16k EPROM with dual 8-bit I/O, the 8251A, a serial communications device, the 8253 timer, the 8255 parallel port, the 8257 DMA controller, the 8259 interrupt controller, and the 8279 keyboard/display interface. Many of these support chips were applied in the original IBM pc, which used a 16-bit processor (the 8088) with 8-bit external interface.

Courtesy, cpushack.com

The 8257 chip handled 4 channels of prioritized direct memory access, and was expandable. It later found applications in the original IBM pc architecture, as the 8088 CPU was 16 bits internally, but had 8-bit external data paths. The 8257 could transfer 16k bytes without CPU intervention. It's internal address and word count registers needed to be initialized by the CPU. It used a word count = 0 interrupt to signal the CPU that the transfer was complete.

The 8085 found use in several space missions, including NASA's OSS series. It was also used on the 1997 JPL Mars Pathfinder Rover Sojourner. This Rover didn't stray far from its lander. The attitude control system on NASA's WIRE spacecraft used an 80C85, as did the FAST and XTE missions.

Zilog Z-80

The Z-80 was designed by Frederico Faggin after he left Intel, and released in 1976. While at Intel, Faggin designed or led the design teams for all of Intel's early processors: the 4004, the 8008, and the 8080. The Z-80 had 8,500 transistors, and could operate at 2.5 MHz. Major advantages of the chip included single power supply operation, and a simplified clock. A non-maskable interrupt (NMI) was added, correcting an oversight in earlier processors that could enter a state where the only exit was a power-off cycle.

The Z-80 was binary compatible with the 8080. Faggin intended it to be an improved version of the 8080. It could execute all of the 8080 operating codes as well as 80 new instructions (including 1-, 4-, 8-, and 16-bit operations, block I/O, block moves) using some of the unused opcodes in the 8080 set. Because the Z-80 had two sets of data registers, it supported fast context switches. There was an indexed addressing mode. The block transfer, essentially a DMA in software, used the BC register pair as a 16 bit byte counter, the DE pair as the destination pointer, and the HL pair as the source pointer. BC was decremented after each transfer. The LDIR and LDDR instructions implemented the block transfer.

The memory interface was vastly simplified over the 8080's, since the CPU generated its own DRAM refresh signals without requiring external circuitry. There were three interrupt modes, mode 0 being equivalent to the 8080's. Mode 1 was a vector call to location 38 hex, and Mode 2 was an indirect call using the I register plus 8 input bits (from the interrupting device) as a pointer to memory.

There were special versions of the Z-80 architecture by Zilog and Hitachi. The 64180 included dual 16-bit timers, DMA controllers, three serial ports, and a memory management unit. The Z-80 lead to advanced versions, the 64180, Z-180, and Z-280 by Zilog and Hitachi. The 64180 was a Z-80 with DMA, 2 UART's. and dual timers.

The Z-80 flew on numerous space missions, including the popular Shuttle attached payloads on the OSS pallets.

NSC800

National's NSC800 had an extended Z80 instruction set, and was implemented in CMOS technology. It was claimed to operate with 5% of the power of an equivalent 8085. There was a multiplex address/data bus, like the 8085.

Images courtesy, cpushack.com

The NSC800 included an 8-bit refresh counter for use with dynamic memory. The NSC800 support chips included the 810 RAM-I/O-timer, the 830 ROM-I/O, the 6504 4k x -bit SRAM, and the 6515 1kx4 SRAM.

804x/805x

The 8041 and 8042 were meant as slave processors to a main CPU. The 8294 was a data encryption unit based on the 8041. The 8292 was a special purpose GPIB controller (IEEE-488 bus).

Photos courtesy, cpushack.com

The 8048 was designed to be a microcontroller, with data storage on-chip. It had single byte instructions, stored in external ROM. It included 64 bytes of RAM, and 27 I/O lines. Later versions had 1k or 4k of internal ROM. The 8049 model had two timers, and the 8050 had four times the RAM and ROM. The 8748 and 49 had EPROM in place of ROM, so they could be programmed by the customer. These chips eventually ran at 6-11 MHz, and were available in CMOS technology for low power.

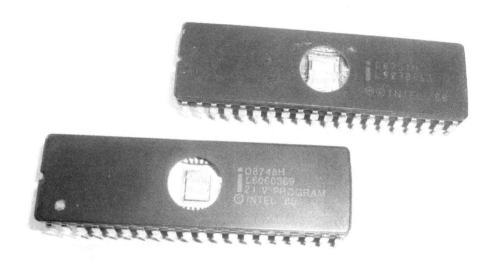

The Intel 8051 was developed from the 8048 as an embedded control processor by Intel in 1980. Embedded processors can operate with fewer external parts, and the 8051 includes memory and Input/Output on the same chip. They had serial I/O plus dual timers, 4k of ROM, and 128 bytes of RAM. They operated up to 16 MHz, and came in ROM-less versions (8031), and in CMOS. The 8044 was an 8051 with a synchronous serial interface to a host machine, and EPROM.

The 8742 was an associated peripheral 8-bit slave microcontroller, meant to be used with the 8051, 8048, and even the 8080 and 8085. It was a follow-on to the 8741 with twice the memory. It was a peripheral chip, but included a complete 8-bit CPU, with 2k of EPROM, 128 bytes of RAM, a clock/timer, and I/O control lines. It was intended to offload I/O from the main CPU. It supported asynchronous transfer with the main processor.

Now, many manufacturers offer versions of the 8051, and it is widely used in college-level embedded systems courses. The most recent instantiations of the design include IP (intellectual property) core versions, for implementation within FPGA's (field programmable gate arrays) that need one or more CPU's. Why re-invent the wheel, when the 8051 comes with a development history, loyal following, and support tools? The 8051 has been used on NASA's environmental satellites Aqua and Aura.

The MOS Technologies 6502

Introduced in 1975, this chip became famous as the engine of the Apple computer. It operated at 1 MHz, and used 4,000 transistors in NMOS technology. It operated from a single 5 volt supply. The earlier 6501 was pin-compatible with Motorola's 6800, not software compatible, but ran into legal problems. Variations included the 6510 with added I/O ports, the 6507 with a reduced 13-bit address bus. The chip was also produced in CMOS technology. It was also used in the Atari and Commodore computers.

The 6522 dual 8-bit parallel port and dual timer chip supported the CPU. The 6502 could also use 6800 peripherals. It allowed for indirect addressing, which neither the 8080 or the 6800 had.

As opposed to most of the other 8-bit CPU designs, the 6502 was little endian. It was limited in registers, having one data register, two index registers, and a stack pointer. It used a PLA for instruction decode and sequencing. Like most microprocessor of the times, the 6502 had undocumented instructions, certain bit patterns that would do strange things. In the 6502's case, the JAM instruction would cause the CPU to freeze, requiring a hard reset. The 6502 remains a popular architecture, and 16 bit and CMOS variations were developed. It was second-sourced by GTE, Rockwell, and NCR. At the time, the same architecture implemented by different manufacturers had different behavior for the same undocumented instructions. This was exciting, but limited code portability.

Rockwell's R6501 was a 6502 CPU plus 2k of ROM, 64 bits of RAM. It could be obtained with a FORTH language compiler in ROM.

The Motorola 6800

The Motorola 6800 chip was introduced in 1975, their first microprocessor. A much simpler architecture than the Intel chips, it had 72 instructions (197 separate opocdes, with the 7 addressing modes), and a single 16-bit index register, but two accumulators. There were one to three bytes per instruction. It ran at 1 MHz, and used 4,100 transistors. The first 6800's were made with what was called "enhancement-mode" NMOS. The problems with this were that it limited the maximum speed (the first chips were 1 MHz) and the die size was quite large. With a large die size there is more likely a fault in the raw silicon wafer within any one die and less die's fit on one wafer. This lead Motorola to have yield problems. Later chips were built with something called "depletion-mode" NMOS which although it upped the transistor count of any design quite significantly, still resulted in a smaller die size and also allowed faster operation.

The 6800's clock was much simpler than the 8080's. There were two clock phases in quadrature, which allowed two chips to be operated in different phases in a type of multiprocessor. The MC6870 provided the simple 2-phase clock. The index register modified operand addresses during execution, typically for vector/array operations. Before index registers and without indirect addressing, array operations were complicated to implement. All I/O was memory-mapped. The 6800 was a synchronous design, so it couldn't wait for long, or easily be used with dynamic memory (because of the refresh cycle). The single index register was sometimes a programming bottleneck.

During development, the Motorola team made a functional 6800 cpu from 450 discrete TTL chips. The

6800 was the first in a family of microprocessors and support chips. It had 8-bit wide data, and a 16-bit wide address bus. It only required a single 5-volt power supply, and used a simple two-phase clock source. It was a synchronous design, so the clock could not be stopped or changed. It had a problem WAIT-ing for an external operation. A machine cycle was defined as a Phase 1 and a Phase 2 clock. During Phase 1, the address for the instruction fetch was placed on the bus. During Phase 2, the instruction was read. On the next Phase 1, the instruction was executed. There were two sets of accumulators, A and B. The status register contained bits to indicate carry/borrow, overflow, zero, negative, and half-carry, as well as an interrupt mask. Upon reset, the 6800 resumed execution with the program counter loaded from the highest memory address.

All interrupts were vectored. The 6800 included a non-maskable interrupt. This fetched the contents from memory addresses FFFC and FFFD into the program counter, effectively forcing a jump to the contents of those addresses. The NMI was the highest priority interrupt. Interrupts were always serviced after the completion of the currently executing instruction. The normal interrupt vectored through locations FFF8 and

74

FFF9. The 6800 had a software interrupt instruction. Executing this instruction was just like an external interrupt occurring. The difference was, it was synchronous to program execution. The program vectored through locations FFFA and FFFB. The RESET signal can be considered an interrupt. With a positive going edge on the reset line, program accessible registers were cleared, and hardware was initialized. The interrupt mask bit was then set, locking out other interrupts. Then the machine vectors through memory locations FFFE and FFFF. There was also a WAIT instruction that caused the processor to stop processing and wait for a hardware interrupt.

Control signals were relatively simple. The VMA line indicated a valid memory address on the address bus. The R/W signal indicated whether the bus was doing a read or write operation. BA indicated the bus was available, as the processor had tri-stated its data and address bus and control lines. An Enable signal was available from ANDing Phase1 of the clock, and the VMA signal.

Some of the associated peripherals included the 6810 128 byte RAM, the 6820/21 PIA dual 8-bit parallel I/O port, the 6828 priority interrupt controller, the 6830 1024 byte ROM, and the 6840 programmable timer module. The 6843 was a floppy disk controller, the 6844 was the DMA controller chip, and the 6845 was a popular video controller, used in the early IBM pc's. The 6850 ACIA was the serial I/O chip (UART). The 6852 was the synchronous serial chip. The 6875 was the clock source.

The 6801 was a microcontroller with the 8-bit CPU, 2k of ROM, a timer, serial port, and 128 bytes of RAM. It included some 16-bit arithmetic instructions, and had a new instruction that would add the B accumulator to the index register. It executed 6800 instructions faster than the 6800, and had 10 new instructions. The 6801 could use external memory. It could do double precision add, subtract, and multiply using pairs of registers. The 6801L1 version had a prom-based version of Motorola's LiLbug debugger.

The 68120 intelligent peripheral controller was a variation of the 6801 with the same RAM and ROM, full duplex UART, and 21 I/O lines. The interface between the peripheral controller and the main CPU was via the on-chip dual-ported RAM. Six semaphore registers were used to control access to the RAM. Because there was no atomic test-and-set mechanism, it was possible that both the host and the peripheral could get different data, as the semaphore is set upon read. In that case, the co-ordination mechanism was that the host would see the semaphore as set, and the peripheral would see it as clear, upon simultaneous read.

The 6802 was a baseline 6800 with 128 bytes of RAM, and an integral clock oscillator. This reduced the number of additional chips required in simple embedded controller applications. The 6802 had 2 Kbytes of ROM, 128 bytes of RAM, 31 parallel I/O lines, 3 serial lines, and triple 16-bit timers. This chip was used by General

Motors in their automobiles. The 6803 was the 6801, less the ROM. The 68701 had EPROM instead of ROM. The 6808 was used in Heath Company's *Hero Robot*, and was a 6800 with clock, but no ROM or RAM.

Photos courtesy, cpushack.com

Photo courtesy, cpushack.com

The 6805 was a microcontroller targeted to the automobile industry. It included bit test operations.

Photo courtesy, cpushack.com

The 6811 was a follow-on chip that featured 16 bit registers and a 16-bit multiply. Radiation hardened versions of the 68HC11 are used in communication satellites. Regular versions are found as embedded controllers in bar code readers, hotel electronic locks, and robots. The HC11 model has an additional Y index register. There was an 8 x 8 multiply, and a 16 by 16 divide. Hitachi's 6309 chip extended the operations to allow four of the 8-bit registers to be used together as a 32-bit register. The 68HC12 was an enhanced version of the HC11. It operated up to 25 MHz, and had 512 kbytes of flash, and 8 kB of RAM.

Photo courtesy, cpushack.com

The 6800 was second-sourced by AMI, Hitachi, Fairchild, Rockwell, and Thomson. Low-power CMOS versions of the CPU and support chips were available from Hitachi. The 6811 and 6812 microcontroller chips are still produced by Freescale Semiconductor (successor to Motorola) and are available as VHDL IP cores

The 6809

The 6809 was an extension to the 6800 architecture, with some 16-bit features. The two 8-bit accumulators could be used together as a single 16-bit register. There were two index registers and two stack pointers. The source code for the 6809 and 6800 was the same, but the 6809 hardware only had 59 instructions. Dropped 6800 instructions were implemented by new instruction pairs. The instructions were translated by the assembler. The 6800 auto-increment and auto-decrement addressing modes allowed easy implementation of a stack machine architecture.

The 6809 had a major feature, an unsigned 8x8 bit multiply instruction, that could extend in to 16-bit and larger word sizes. There were also more addressing modes, and a built-in clock. The 6809 supported cycle-steal dynamic memory access. One major difference from the 6800 was that the 6809's stack pointer pointed to the last item in the stack not the next empty location, as in the 6800. That was an increment and store operation in place of store and increment. There were two stack pointers, to be used for code and data. The 6809 continued the tradition of not causing a fault (interrupt) on attempted execution of undefined opcodes. This simplified the decoding logic, but could not respond to attempted execution of data. Second sources were AMI, Hitachi, Fujitsu, Fairchild, Rockwell, and Thompson.

6839 Floating Point ROM

Motorola's 6839 chip was an 8k x 8 ROM, containing binary floating point support software for the 6809. This was an attempt to furnish off-the-shelf plug-in code for 6809 system developers. The code was designed to be position independent and reentrant. Using no absolute addresses, it was easily integrated anywhere into the address space. It implemented the entire IEEE Proposed Standard for Floating Point, version 8. This included the basic math operations, comparisons, and conversions. Operands could be put on the hardware stack, or passed in registers. Both 16 and 32 bit integers were supported, as well as BCD strings. The 6839 was the only code-in-rom chip developed by Motorola.

IMP-8

This was a National Semiconductor CPU that operated at 715 KHz, and was built in PMOS technology. It was the 8-bit part of a family that also included 4-bit, 12-bit, and eventually 16-bit versions. The IMP-8 was replaced by the COP-8 model.

SC/MP

This National Semiconductor CPU, a single chip micro processor, was developed for embedded control applications. It operated at 1 MHz, implemented in

PMOS technology. A major feature of the architecture was that multiple processors could share the system bus.

Signetics 2650

This circa-1975 chip operated at 1.2 MHz, and was implemented in NMOS. There was an accumulator and 6 other registers. It had an on-chip subroutine stack.

Photo courtesy, cpushack.com

Signetics 8X300

The 8X300 was somewhat different in being implemented in bipolar, not MOS technology. It was an 8-bit unit, developed as a second-source of the SMS-300 from Scientific Micro Systems. The different technology gave the unit a significant speed advantage, at the cost of high power consumption. It used an 8 MHz clock. There was a dedicated 13 bit address bus for 16-bit wide program memory. A separate 8 bit data/address bus was used for data access and I/O.

The instruction set allowed for direct manipulation of bits within a word. In addition to the standard ALU, there was a rotate unit for data bytes, and a shift-merge unit. One application of the 8x300, subject of an ApNote from Signetics, was as a floppy disk controller.

RCA 1802

CDP 1801 was a 2-chip set, circa 1975. It operated at 2MHz, using 5,000 transistors, in CMOS technology. The 1800 series processors from RCA were designed by Joe Weisbecker. The 1801's separate chips represented the ALU and the control unit. The 1801 operated up to 4 MHz. It had 59 instructions. The registers could be viewed as 8 or 16 bits in width.

The 1802 was released by RCA in 1976. It was quite a different architecture than other contemporary CPU's, and was produced in complementary metal oxide semiconductor (CMOS) technology, which is both low-power and radiation resistant, though susceptible to electrostatic discharge. It was also a static logic design, which could operate at a wide range of clock speeds down to zero. The architecture has also been implemented in silicon-on-sapphire technology which greatly improved its radiation hardness. It operated at up to 6.4 MHz.

1802's were found in Chrysler Corporation's electronic ignition units for their gas engines, video games, video terminals, and the ELF computer. There was a broad family of support chips, including the 1855 multiply/divide coprocessor. The 1804 was an 1802 with 2 KB of ROM and 32 bytes of RAM.

Photo courtesy, cpushack.com

The 1802 had a register file of 16 registers of 16 bits each. Using the SEP instruction, one could select any of the registers to be the program counter or index register. It also used 16-bit addressing. Support chips included the 1852 8-bit I/O port, the 1854 UART, the 1856 memory buffer, and the 1857 I/O buffer.

A few commonly used subroutines could be called quickly by keeping their address in one of the 16 registers. Before a subroutine returned, it jumped to the location immediately preceding its entry point so that after the RET instruction returned control to the caller, the register would be pointing to the right value for next time. An interesting variation was to have two or more subroutines in a ring so that they were called in round-robin order.

The RCA 1802 was one of the first RISC chips. RISC (Reduced Instruction Chip Computer) refers to an optimization technique where the instruction set is streamlined for performance. However, it makes the chip more difficult to program.

Radiation hardened versions of the 1802, developed by Sandia, were used on JPL's Voyager, Viking, and Galileo space probes. It was the first microprocessor to fly in space, on the Oscar satellite, in 1978.

Fairchild F8

The F8 was introduced in 1975 by Fairchild Semiconductor. It was their first microprocessor. One of the chief designers was Robert Noyce, who went on to found Intel Corporation. Interestingly, the processor had no stack pointer, program counter, nor address bus. Addresses were maintained in the address pointer register. The chip also had 64 bytes of scratchpad memory and 64 registers. It was initially produced as a two-chip version, with a single chip implementation by Mostek in 1977. The 2-chip version did not need additional support chips; the associated 3851 was a ROM. It's clock was 2 MHz, and it was implemented in an NMOS process. There were 71 instructions, and 64 general purpose registers on the chip itself, serving as RAM.

The chip was targeted to embedded applications in areas such as gas pumps, vending machines, and cash registers. It was second-sourced by Mostek.

The F8 also found application onboard NASA's Payload Assist Module (PAM-D), an upper stage for the Space Shuttle payloads, allowing the shuttle to launch a payload into a geosynchronous or higher orbit. The PAM-D was a Delta-class solid-fuel module, providing the same performance to higher orbit as a Delta rocket launched from the ground. Since the operation of the PAM on orbit was only a matter of minutes, the usual issues of radiation damage were not all that applicable.

Other 8-bit examples include the PPS-8 by Rockwell, operating at 256 KHz, in a PMOS technology. There was also the Burroughs Mini-D, a 1 MHz PMOS multi-chip.

Mostek 3850

The Mostek 3850 combined two earlier Fairchild chips into one, and was released in 1977. It was based on the F8 architecture, with RAM and I/O.

TMS-7000

The TMS-7000 was introduced in 1981 as an 8-bit follow-on to Texas Instrument's TMS-1000 4-bit processor. Like the TMS-1000, they included ROM and RAM, and featured a user-definable instruction set. For microcontroller use, they included 128 bits or 256 bits of RAM, and either no ROM, 2k of ROM, or 4 k of ROM. The chip had up to 3 timers, serial I/O, and 32 I/O lines. They could be ordered in an EPROM version for prototyping, and a CMOS version was available as well.

Contemporary 8-bit processors

There are still jobs an 8-bit processor can do well. Existing code that is proven correct can be re-used on newer but functionally equivalent hardware. Sometimes, 8-bits gets the job done, with less power and smaller size than 16 bits. Thus, 8-bit processors have survived, and new ones continue to appear. The Intel 8051 and Zilog Z-80 still exist in many variations and as an IP (Intellectual Property) core for implementation in FPGA's. Atmel also makes 8051 variants. Freescale Semiconductor has their Motorola 8-bit clones, the 68HC08 and -11. PIC has a full line of embedded 8-bit processors. Other company's such as Atmel and NEC have similar products as well.

Zilog Z-8

The Zilog Z-8 was introduced in 1979. It is a load-store architecture, different in concept from the Z-80 chip. It was marketed as an embedded processor.

The chip survives today as the eZ series. On chip RAM can be used as up to 4096 registers. A 16-bit address space for ROM or flash is provided. A variety of models in the family include different combinations of I/O such as A/D, SPI and I^2C interfaces, and there are multiple packaging options.

Microchip PIC 8-bit Microcontrollers

The 8-bit line of microcontrollers is helpfully called the PIC16. These come with a variety of memory types and sizes, and I/O options. They operate at a frequency of 20

MHz. They do have separate instruction and data busses (Harvard architecture) with simultaneous access. The simplest model has no interrupts, but single or multiple interrupt models are available. Data memory, on chip, starts at 138 bytes. Program memory starts at 3 KB. PIC originally stood for peripheral interface controller. The PIC processors come in numerous variations, and have a large register set.

Atmel AVR

AVR makes a modern 8-bit microcontroller in a RISC architecture. It is a fully static architecture, meaning the clock can be slowed and stopped, without loss of state. It can operate at 16 MHz, and includes hardware multiplication. There are 130 instructions, and 32 registers. It includes 64 Kbytes of flash memory, and 2 Kbytes of EEPROM, with 4 k bytes of SRAM. It can also address additional external memory. The chip is more than the equivalent of a previous 8-bit generation board.

The AVR includes two 8-bit counter-timers, two 16-bit counter-timers, a real-time counter, dual 8-bit pulse-width modulation registers, up to six 16-bit PWM channels, eight 10-bit ADC's, dual serial UARTS, SPI interface, and an analog comparator. The clock frequency is selectable by software.

Atmega 64

The Atmega64 is an 8-bit microcontroller with 64 kbytes of flash memory. It can operated up to 16 MHz, and also includes 4k of SRAM, and 2K of EEPROM. It has an 8-bit counter-timer, an 8-channel PWM, 53 I/O lines, 8 interrupts, 2 serial channels, and an 8-channel, 10-bit A/D. The Atmega128 has twice the flash memory.

HuC6280

The HuC6280 8-bit microprocessor is Japanese company, Hudson Soft's, improved version of the WDC 65C02 CPU, an upgraded CMOS version of the popular NMOS-based MOS Technology 6502 8-bit CPU. The HuC6280 contains a 65C02 core which has several additional instructions and a few internal peripheral functions such as an interrupt controller, a memory management unit, a timer, an 8-bit parallel I/O port, and a programmable sound generator. The processor operates at two speeds, 1.79 MHz and 7.16 MHz.

Electronic Arrays 9002

The EA9002 was intended as a competitor to the Fairchild F8 and RCA 1802, but was late to production and market, and never gained popularity. It was flexible in allowing the use of either Intel or Motorola support chips. It had a four kilobyte address space, and used a 4MHz clock. There were 58 instructions, with 8 general purpose registers, and seven vectored interrupts.

Western Digital MP1600

The 1600 was implemented with 3 chips, and was microprogrammable. The 1611 was the ALU with 26 registers and an accumulator. The 1621 was the control unit. The micro-program was stored in the 1631 ROM. With a different ROM, the chipset could become a 16-bit machine, and formed a DEC LSI-11, with the PDP-11 instruction set.

The 12-bit micro

We'll extend the discussion just a little to include 12-bit processors. Probably the best known 12-bit architecture example is the circa 1965 DEC PDP-8 minicomputer. The CPU in this unit was a board of DTL flip-chips, not a monolithic 12-bit processor. But, the instruction set was popular. I liked the PDP-8, and learned to program it as an undergrad.

6100A

The 6100A from Harris Corp. was a 1975 12-bit microprocessor and associated peripherals and memory. The chip used the DEC PDP-8 instruction set with 90 single word instructions. It had a program counter register, a 12-bit accumulator, AC, and an MQ register (for multiply and divide operations). As there was no stack, subroutine return addresses were stored in the first word of the subroutine. Conditionals allowed the next instruction to be skipped. There was one maskable interrupt. At interrupt, the CPU stored the current address at location zero in memory, and jumped indirectly through address one. The chip was a static design.

Photos   courtesy,
cpushack.com

Limited to 4096 words of memory by the 12-bit architecture, the 6100 architecture was extended by the associated 6102. This added three address lines, for a total of 32k words, by paging. It also supported DMA, and added a timer. The 6101 Parallel Interface Element (PIE) chip was an I/O port. It had dual, 12-bit input and output ports. Up to 31 of the chips per system could be used. The 6103 was a parallel I/O device with DMA, that could be used to refresh DRAM. All of these chips had their own unique instructions. The 6402 was a UART. Intersil provided matching SRAM (12-bits) and PROM.

The 6120 was a higher performance 6100, and the 6121 was the associated I/O controller.

The 6100 was built in CMOS technology. It was low-power, and widely used in high-reliability applications. It was available in military-spec versions, and was dual sourced by Intersil. The maximum clock speed was 8 MHz. another advantage of the CMOS implementation was the ability to operate from a single voltage source, in the range of 4-11 volts.

The chip found itself in a DEC-produced personal computer, the DECmate. The chip was sold for commercial use through 1982. It was also used on instruments on NASA's Solar Maximum Mission (SMM) spacecraft, launched in 1980.

The 1974 Toshiba TLCS-12 was also a 12-bit CPU, operating at 1 MHz, implemented in NMOS.

The MCP-1600 was a Western Digital multichip set from the late 1970's. It was used for the DEC LSI-11, and the Pascal MicroEngine. It had a control chip, a register/ALU, and one to four ROM chips. It was an 8-bit CPU, that could do 16-bit arithmetic.

And, in conclusion….

Modern computers started out using relays and vacuum tubes, switching to mechanical relays for switching elements. The semiconductor revolution provided diodes for logic functions, and transistors for switching. As the technology allowed for putting multiple transistors and other elements on a single substrate, the integrated circuit began to be widely used. The complexity of the devices increased according to an exponential growth law, the technology feeding upon itself. This allowed for functions such as an arithmetic-logic unit to occupy one chip. Then, at around 4,000 transistors capacity, an entire 4-bit CPU that executed instructions. Not much later came the 8-bit CPU. Memory and I/O functions also benefited from the increasingly complex solid state-electronics. The next step along the way was the 16-bit processor.

Bit slice

1's complement – a binary number representation scheme for negative values.

2's complement – another binary number representation scheme for negative values.

2-wire – twisted pair wire channel for full duplex communications. Still needs a common ground.

Accumulator – a register to hold numeric values during and after an operation.

ACM – Association for Computing Machinery; professional organization.

ALU – arithmetic logic unit.

Analog – concerned with continuous values.

AND – logical operation on data. Output is true, if and only if both inputs are true

ANSI – American National Standards Institute

Arduino – open source, single board microcontroller using an Atmel AVR (8-bit RISC) CPU.

ASCII - American Standard Code for Information Interchange, a 7-bit code; developed for teleprinters.

Assembly language – low level programming language specific to a particular ISA.

Async – asynchronous; using different clocks.

Baud – symbol rate; may or may not be the same as bit rate.

Baudot – a five-bit code used with teleprinters.

BCD – binary coded decimal. 4-bit entity used to represent 10 different decimal digits; with 6 spare states.

Big-endian – data format with the most significant bit or byte at the lowest address, or transmitted first.

Binary – using base 2 arithmetic for number representation.

BIST – built-in self test.

Bit – smallest unit of digital information; two states.

Blackbox – functional device with inputs and outputs, but no detail on the internal workings.

Boolean – a data type with two values; an operation on these data types; named after George Boole, mid-19th century inventor of Boolean algebra.

Borrow – mathematical operation when a digit become smaller than limit and the deficiency is taken from the next digit to the left.

Buffer – a temporary holding location for data.

Bug – an error in a program or device.

Bus – data channel, communication pathway for data transfer.

Byte – ordered collection of 8 bits; values from 0-255

Cache – faster and smaller intermediate memory between the processor and main memory.

Carry – arithmetic result, when a digit is larger than a limit and the extra is moved to the left.

CAS – column address strobe (in DRAM refreshing)

Chip – integrated circuit component.

Clock – periodic timing signal to control and synchronize operations.

CMOS – complementary metal oxide semiconductor; a technology using both positive and negative semiconductors to achieve low power operation.

Complement – in binary logic, the opposite state.

Control Flow – computer architecture involving directed flow through the program; data dependent paths are allowed.

Coprocessor – another processor to supplement the operations of the main processor. Used for floating point, video, etc. Usually relies on the main processor for instruction fetch; and control.

Core – early non-volatile memory technology based on ferromagnetic toroid's.

Cots – commercial, off-the-shelf.

CPU – central processing unit.

DCE – data communications equipment; interface to the network.

DEC – Digital Equipment Corporation.

DEMUX – demultiplex.

Digital – using discrete values for representation of states or numbers.

DMA - direct memory access (to/from memory, for I/O devices).

Double word – two words; if word = 8 bits, double word = 16 bits.

DRAM – dynamic random access memory.

Drum memory – obsolete storage media using large cylindrical magnetic media.

DTE – data terminal equipment; communicates with the DCE to get to the network.

DTL – diode-transistor logic

EEPROM – electrically erasable PROM

EIA – Electronics Industry Association.

Embedded system – a computer systems with limited human interfaces and performing specific tasks. Usually part of a larger system.

Epitaxial – in semiconductors, have a crystalline overlayer with a well-defined orientation.

EPROM – erasable programmable read-only memory.

EEPROM – electrically erasable read-only memory.

Exception – interrupt due to internal events, such as overflow.

Fail-safe – a system designed to do no harm in the event of failure.

FET – field effect transistor.

Fetch/execute cycle – basic operating cycle of a computer; fetch the instruction, execute the instruction.

Firmware – code contained in a non-volatile memory.

Fixed point – computer numeric format with a fixed number of digits or bits, and a fixed radix point. Integers.

Flag – a binary indicator.

Flip-flop – a circuit with two stable states; ideal for binary.

Floating point – computer numeric format for real numbers; has significant digits and an exponent.

FPGA – field programmable gate array.

FPU – floating point unit, an ALU for floating point numbers.

Full duplex – communication in both directions simultaneously.

Gate – a circuit to implement a logic function; can have multiple inputs, but a single output.

GUI – graphical user interface.

Half-duplex – communications in two directions, but not simultaneously.

Handshake – co-ordination mechanism.

Harvard architecture – memory storage scheme with separate instructions and data.

HCF – Motorola 6800/6809 undocumented instruction, Halt and Catch Fire.

Hexadecimal – base 16 number representation.

Hexadecimal point – radix point that separates integer from fractional values of hexadecimal numbers.

HP – Hewlett-Packard Company. Instrumentation and computers.

IEEE – Institute of Electrical and Electronic Engineers. Professional organization and standards body.

IEEE-754 – standard for floating point representation and operations.

Index register – register to hold an address.

Infinity - the largest number that can be represented in the number system.

Integer – the natural numbers, zero, and the negatives of the natural numbers.

Interrupt – an external asynchronous event to signal a need for attention (example: the phone rings).

Interrupt vector – entry in a table pointing to an interrupt service routine; indexed by interrupt number.

I/O – Input-output from the computer to external devices, or a user interface.

IP – intellectual property; also internet protocol.

IP core – IP describing a chip design that can be licensed to be used in an FPGA or ASIC.

ISA – instruction set architecture, the software description of the computer.

ISO – International Standards Organization.

ISR – interrupt service routine, a subroutine that handles a particular interrupt event.

JTAG – Joint Test Action Group; industry group that lead to IEEE 1149.1, Standard Test Access Port and Boundary-Scan Architecture.

Junction – in semiconductors, the boundary interface of the n-type and p-type material.

Kilo – a prefix for 10^3 or 2^{10}

Ladder logic – description of relay-based logic circuits. Obsolete.

Latency – time delay.

Little-endian – data format with the least significant bit or byte at the highest address, or transmitted last.

Logic operation – generally, negate, AND, OR, XOR, and their inverses.

LSB – least significant bit or byte.

LSI – large scale integration

Machine language – native code for a particular computer hardware.

Mainframe – a computer you can't lift.

Mantissa – significant digits (as opposed to the exponent) of a floating point value.

Master-slave – control process with one element in charge. Master status may be exchanged among elements.

Math operation – generally, add, subtract, multiply, divide.

Mega - 10^6 or 2^{20}

MHz – megahertz, one million cycles per second.

Microcode – hardware level data structures to translate machine instructions into sequences of circuit level operations.

Microcontroller – microprocessor with included memory and/or I/O.

Microprocessor – a monolithic CPU on a chip.

Microprogramming – modifying the microcode,

Minicomputer – smaller than a mainframe, larger than a pc.

MIPS – millions of instructions per second; sometimes used as a measure of throughput.

Modem – modulator/demodulator; digital communications interface for analog channels.

MSB – most significant bit or byte.

Multiplex – combining signals on a communication channel by sampling.

Mux - multiplex

NAN – not-a-number; invalid bit pattern.

NAND – negated (or inverse) AND function.

NASA – National Aeronautics and Space Administration.

NDA – non-disclosure agreement; legal agreement protecting IP.

Negate – logical operation on data; changes the state.

Nibble – 4 bits, ½ byte.

NIST – National Institute of Standards and Technology (US), previously, National Bureau of Standards.

NMI – non-maskable interrupt; cannot be ignored by the software.

NMOS – negative metal oxide semiconductor.

NOR – negated (or inverse) OR function

Normalized number – in the proper format for floating point representation.

NRE – non-recurring engineering; one-time costs for a project.

Null modem – acting as two modems, wired back to back. Artifact of the RS-232 standard.

NVM – non-volatile memory.

Nxor – logical operation on data; negated XOR.

Nyquist rate – in communications, the minimum sampling rate, equal to twice the highest frequency in the signal.

Octal – base 8 number.

Off-the-shelf – commercially available; not custom.

Opcode – part of a machine language instruction that specifies the operation to be performed.

OR – logical operation on data; output is true if either or both inputs are true.

Overflow - the result of an arithmetic operation exceeds the capacity of the destination.

Paradigm – a pattern or model

Paradigm shift – a change from one paradigm to another. Disruptive or evolutionary.

Parallel – multiple operations or communication proceeding simultaneously.

Parity – an error detecting mechanism involving an extra check bit in the word.

PC – personal computer, politically correct, program counter.

PCB – printed circuit board.

Pic – a microcontroller from Microchip Technology.

Pinout – mapping of signals to I/O pins of a device.

PLC – Programmable logic controller, embedded device f   or automation.

PLD– programmable logic device; generic gate-level part that can be programmed for a function.

Pooling – periodic checking

PROM – programmable read-only memory.

PMOS – positive metal oxide semiconductor.

PWM – pulse width modulation – digital technique for motor control.

Quad word – four words. If word = 16 bits, quad word is 64 bits.

Queue – first in, first out data buffer structure; hardware of software.

Rad – unit of absorbed radiation dose; 100 ergs per gram; also, radian, angular measurement.

Radix point – separates integer and fractional parts of a real number.

RALU – registers and arithmetic logic unit

RAM – random access memory; any item can be access in the same time as any other.

RAS – Row address strobe, in DRAM refresh.

Register – temporary storage location for a data item.

Reset – signal and process that returns the hardware to a known, defined state.

RISC – reduced instruction set computer.

ROM – read only memory.

Real-time – system that responds to events in a predictable, bounded time.

Refresh – restore the contents of DRAM.

Register – small, fast memory for storing intermediate and temporary results.

RS-232 – EIA telecommunications standard (1962), serial with handshake.

SAM – sequential access memory, like a magnetic tape.

Self-modifying code – computer code that modifies itself as it run; hard to debug

Semiconductor – material with electrical characteristics between conductors and insulators; basis of current technology processor and memory devices.

Semaphore –signaling element among processes.

Serial – bit by bit.

Seu – single event upset; radiation induced upset in a device.

Shift – move one bit position to the left or right in a word.

Sign-magnitude – number representation with a specific sign bit.

Signed number – representation with a value and a numeric sign.

SOC – system on chip

SoS – silicon on Sapphire (substrate)

Software – set of instructions and data to tell a computer what to do.

SRAM – static random access memory.

Stack – first in, last out data structure. Can be hardware or software.

Stack pointer – a reference pointer to the top of the stack.

State machine – model of sequential processes.

Synchronous – using the same clock to coordinate operations.

System – a collection of interacting elements and relationships with a specific behavior.

Test-and-set – coordination mechanism for multiple processes that allows reading to a location and writing it in a non-interruptible manner.

TCP/IP – transmission control protocol/internet protocol; layered set of protocols for networks.

TMR – Triple Modular Redundancy; an error control mechanism using redundant components.

Transceiver – receiver and transmitter in one box.

TRAP – exception or fault handling mechanism in a computer; an operating system component.

Triplicate – using three copies (of hardware, software, messaging, power supplies, etc.). for redundancy and error control.

Tristate logic – has two logic states, plus an "off" or high impedance state.

Truncate – discard. Cutoff, make shorter.

TTL – transistor-transistor logic in digital integrated circuits. (1963)

UART – universal asynchronous receiver-transmitter. Parallel-to-serial; serial-to parallel device with handshaking.

USART – universal synchronous (or) asynchronous receiver/transmitter.

Underflow – the result of an arithmetic operation is smaller than the smallest representable number.

USAF – United States Air Force.

Unsigned number – a number without a numeric sign.

UvPROM – field programmable memory that can be erased by exposure to ultraviolet light.

Vector – single dimensional array of values.

VHDL- very high level description language; a language to describe integrated circuits and asic/ fpga's.

Via – vertical conducting pathway through an insulating layer in a semiconductor.

Von Neumann, John, a computer pioneer and mathematician; realized that computer instructions are data.

Watchdog – hardware/software function to sanity check the hardware, software, and process; applies corrective action if a fault is detected; fail-safe mechanism.

Wiki – the Hawaiian word for "quick." Refers to a collaborative content website.

Word – a collection of bits of any size; does not have to be a power of two.

Write-only – of no interest.

XOR – exclusive OR; either but not both.

Zener – voltage reference diode.

Zero address – architecture using implicit addressing, like a stack.

Bibliography

General

Artwick, Bruce A. *Microcomputer Interfacing*, 1980, Prentice-Hall, ISBN 0135809029.

Ganssle, Jack G. (1992). *The Art of Programming Embedded Systems*. San Diego: Academic Press. p. 13. ISBN 978-0-12-274880-6.

Gaonkar, Ramesh S. *Microprocessor Architecture, Programing, and Applications with the 8085*, 4th ed, 1999, Prentice-Hall, ISBN 0139012575.

Osborne, Adam *4 & 8 bit Microprocessors Handbook*, 1981, Osborne McGraw Hill, ISBN 0079310427.

Osborne, Adam *An Introduction to Microcomputers*, Osborne-McGraw Hill, 1980, ISBN 0-931988-34-9.

Predko, Michael. 1999. *Handbook of Microcontrollers*. New York: McGraw-Hill/Tab, 1998, ISBN- 0079137172.

Rafiquzzaman, Mohamed. *Microprocessors: Theory and Applications* (Intel and Motorola), Englewood Cliffs, N.J. Prentice Hall, 1992, ISBN 0135881463.

Stuart R. Ball. (2002). *Embedded Microprocessor Systems Real World Design*. Amsterdam: Newnes. p. 34. ISBN 978-0-7506-7534-5.

Wagner, Terry John *Fundamentals of Microcomputer Programming* Macmillan, 1984. ISBN 0024237108.

1-bit

Gregory, Vern *MC14500B Industrial Control Unit Handbook,* 1977, Motorola, ASIN: B0006XCOPK.

Motorola Semiconductor, Industrial Control Unit, MC14500B, 1994.

4004/4040

Myslewski, Rik *Happy 40th Birthday Intel 4004*, The Register, December 15, 2011, Amazon Digital Services, Inc.. ASIN: B006MSQKOE.

Westbeck, Staffan *Program development on a PDP-11 system for Intel micro Computer 8008 and 4004,* 1974, Stockholm, Technical report / Telecommunication Theory, Electrical Engineering, Royal Institute of Technology, ISSN: 0346-8879.

Busicom 141-PF calculator and the Intel 4004 microprocessor, http://www.vintagecalculators.com/html/busicom_141-pf_and_intel_4004.html

http://www.intel4004.com

http://www.intel.com/Assets/PDF/DataSheet/4004_datas
heet.pdf

8008/8080/8085/Z-80/NSC800

Anderson, J. S. *Microprocessor Technology*, 2012, Taylor & Francis, ISBN 9781136078064.

Barden, William *The Z-80 Microcomputer Handbook*, 1978, Sams, ISBN 0672215004.

Boyet, H. 8085 Microprocessor, Motilal UK Books of India, 2010, ISBN-10: 8183333737.

Coffron, James W. *Practical Hardware Details for 8080, 8085, Z80 and 6800 Microprocessor Systems*, 1981, Prentice Hall, ISBN- 0136910890.

Cohn, David L. *A Step by Step Introduction to 8080 Microprocessor Systems,* Dilithium Press, 1977, ISBN- 0918398045.

Maples, Michael D. *Floating Point Package for Intel 8008 and 8080 Microprocessors,* Oct. 24, 1975, Lawrence Livermore Lab, University of California.

Gaonkar, Ramesh S. *The Z80 Microprocessor: Architecture, Interfacing, and Design*, 1992, 2nd ed, Merrill Publishing Co. ISBN 0023404841.

Intel, Embedded Controller Handbook, (80186, 80188), 1987, 210918.

Intel Microprocessor and Peripheral Handbook, 2 Vol., 1987, 230843.

Kumar, N. Sentil Saravanan, M. and Jeevananthan, S. Microprocessors and Microcontrollers Oxford University Press, USA, 2011, ISBN-10: 0198066473.

Lalond, David *The 8080, 8085, and Z80: Hardware, Software, Programming, Interfacing, and Troubleshooting*, Prentice Hall, 1988,ISBN-013247008X.

Larsen, David G. *8080/8085 Software Design*, Howard W Sams, 1st ed., 1979, ISBN- 0672215411.

Leventhal, Lance *Z80 Assembly language Programming*, 1979, Osborne, ISBN 0931988217.

Maples, Michael D. "Floating-Point Package for Intel 8008 and 8080 Microprocessors,"
UCRL-51940, Lawrence Livermore Laboratory, October 24, 1975.

Osborne, Adam *8080 Programming for Logic Design*, 1976, Sybex, ASIN B00073F4JW.

Osborne, Adam *Z80 Programming for Logic Design,* 1978, Osborne & Associates, McGraw-Hill Osborne Media; 1st ed., 1978, ISBN-10: 093198811X.

Phillips, George M. *The Collector's Guide to Vintage Intel Microchips,* 2006, (CD-ROM), Smithsonian, ISBN 0977239608.

Rony, Peter R. T*he 8080A Bugbook: Microcomputer Interfacing and Programming,* 1977, Sams, ISBN 0672214474.

Uffenbeck, John *Microcomputers and Microprocessors: The 8080, 8085, and Z-80 Programming, Interfacing, and Troubleshooting* (3rd Edition), 1999, Prentice Hall, ISBN 0132091984.

Weller, Shatzel, Nice. *Practical Microcomputer Programming : the Intel 8080,* 1976, ISBN 0930594010.

Winter, Keith *Comparison Study NSC800 vs. 8085 vs. Z80,* National Semiconductor Application Brief, Jan. 1981.

Zaks, Rodnay *Programming the Z-80,* 1981, Sybex, ISBN 0895880695.

The 8080/8085 Microprocessor Book, Intel Corp. 1980, Wiley, ISBN ISBN- 0471035688.

"CPU Control Register". Z80182/Z8L182 Zilog Intelligent Peripheral Controller Product Specification. San Jose, California: Zilog. 1997. pp. 3–48.

Z80180 Microprocessor Unit Product Specification,. San Jose, California: Zilog. November 2006. Retrieved 2009-07-15.

Z80S180/Z80L180 Product Specification, San Jose, California: Zilog. 2000. Retrieved 2009-07-15.

Z8S180 SL1960 Product Specification, San Jose, California: Zilog. 1998. Retrieved 2009-07-15.

Z8018x MPU Family User Manual, San Jose, California: Zilog. 2003.

Mostek, *Z-80 Programming Manual*, 1977.

Intel 8051

Intel 8 bit Embedded Control Handbook, Jan. 92, ISBN 1555121217.

Ayala, Kenneth J. *The 8051 Microcontroller*. 3rd ed. Clifton Park, NY: Thomson Delmar Learning, 2004, ISBN-10: 140186158X.

Ayala, Kenneth J. *8051 Microprocessor: Architecture, Programming, and Applications,* 1997, West Publishing Co. ISBN- 0314772782.

Calcutt, D. M., Frederick J. Cowan, G. Hassan Parchizadeh, *8051 microcontrollers.* Burlington, MA: Newnes.

Ghoshal, Subrata, *8051 microcontroller.* New Delhi, India: Dorling Kindersley and Safari Books Online. 2010.

Karakehayov, Zdravko, Knud Smed Christensen, and Ole Winther. *Embedded systems design with 8051 microcontrollers : Hardware and software.* Electrical Engineering and Electronics. Vol. 108. 1999,New York: Marcel Dekker.

MacKenzie, I. Scott. 1999. *The 8051 microcontroller.* 3rd ed. Upper Saddle River, N.J.: Prentice Hall.

Predko, Mike *Programming and customizing the 8051 microcontroller.* New York: McGraw-Hill/Tab, 1999, ISBN- 0071341927.

Schultz, Thomas W. 1998; 1999. *C and the 8051.* 2nd ed. Upper Saddle River, N.J.: Prentice Hall PTR.

MOS Technologies 6502

Carr, Joseph J. *6502 User's Manual.* Reston, Virginia: Reston Pub. Co., c1984.

DeJong, Marvin L. *Programming & Interfacing the 6502, with Experiments*. Indianapolis, Indiana: Howard W. Sams, Inc., 1980.

Fernandez, Judi N. & Tabler, Donna N. & Ashley, Ruth. *6502 Assembly Language Programming*. New York, New York: John Wiley & Sons, Inc. ISBN 0-471-86120-0.

Findley, Robert. *6502 Software Gourmet Guide and Cookbook*. Elmwood, Connecticut: Scelbi Publications, c1979.

Foster, Caxton C. *Programming a Microcomputer: 6502*. Reading, Massachusetts: Addison-Wesley Pub. Co., c1978.

Holland, John M. *Advanced 6502 Interfacing*. Indianapolis, Indiana: Howard W. Sams, Inc., 1982.

Hyde, Randy. *Using 6502 Assembly Language*. Chatsworth, California: Datamost, Inc., 1981.

Leventhal, Lance A. *6502 Assembly Language Programming*. Berkeley, California: Osborne/McGraw-Hill., 1979. ISBN 0-931988-27-6.

Leventhal, Lance A. & Saville, Winthrop. *6502 Assembly Language Subroutines*. Berkley, California: Osborne McGraw-Hill, 1982.

MCS6500 - Microcomputer Family - Programming Manual. Norristown, Pennsylvania: MOS Publication #6500-50A, 1976.

Overaa, Paul. *Teach Yourself Asssembler 6502*. London, England: Century Communications Ltd, 1985. ISBN 0-7126-0550-9.

Scanlon, Leo J. *6502 Software Design*. Indianapolis, Indiana: Howard W. Sams & Co, Inc., 1980.

Skier, Ken. *Beyond Games: Systems Software for your 6502 Personal Computer*. Petersborough, New Hampshire: Byte Publications, 1981.

Skier, Ken. *Top-Down Assembly Language Programming for the 6502 Personal Computer*. New York, New York: McGraw-Hill Book Co., 1981.

Stephenson, A. P. *6502 Machine Code for Beginners*. Kent, England: Butterworth & Co. Ltd, 1983. ISBN 0-408-01311-7.

Smith, Mike. *6502 Machine and Assembly Language Programming*. Blue Ridge Summit, Pennsylvania: Tab Books, c1984.

Tootill, Alan & Barrow, David. *6502 Machine Code for Humans*. London, Great Britain: Granada Publishing, 1984. ISBN 0-246-12076-2.

Weller, Walter J. *Practical Microcomputer Programming: the 6502*. Evanston, Illinois: Northern Technology Books, c1980. ISBN 0-930594-08-8.

Windeknecht, Thomas G. *6502 Systems Programming*. Boston, Massachusetts: Little, Brown and Co., 1983.

Zaks, Rodnay. *6502 Applications Book*. Berkeley, California: Sybex Inc., 1979. ISBN 0-89588-015-6.

Zaks, Rodnay. *Advanced 6502 Programming*. Berkeley, California: Sybex Inc., 1982. ISBN 0-89588-089-X.

Zaks, Rodnay. *Programming the 6502 (Fourth Edition)*. Berkeley, California: Sybex Inc., 1983. ISBN 0-89588-046-

Motorola 6800

Heathkit/Zenith Educational Systems *Microprocessors: Including Programming Experiments*, 1985. Benton Harbor, Mich., Heath Co.

Osborne, Adam *6800 Programming for Logic Design,* 1977, Osborne & Associates, ASIN B0006CVUUQ.

Lipovski, G. Jack. 1999. *Single and Multi-chip Microcontroller Interfacing : For the Motorola 68HC12*, San Diego, Calif.: Academic Press.

Valvano, Jonathan W. 2003. *Introduction to Embedded Microcomputer Systems \: Motorola 6811 and 6812 simulation.* Pacific Grove, CA: Thomson-Brooks/Cole.

M6800 Application Manual,

http://www.wickensonline.co.uk/hx-20/M6800applMan_Mar75.pdf

Texas Instruments

TMS 1000 Family Design Manual (Microcomputer Series), 1982, Texas Instruments, ASIN B003OOSJ7U.

Misc.

Seiko Epson Corp. S*1C63 Family, Core CPU Manua*l, 2001, MF855-03a.

MARC4 4-bit Microcontrollers Programmer's Guide, Atmel, 2004, document 4747A–4BMCU–01/04.

Fairchild Semiconductor, *PPS-25 Programmable Processor System* (preliminary) User Manual, Oct. 25, 1972.

Bates, Martin P. *Programming 8-bit pic microcontroller in c,* 2008, Newnes, ISBN 0750689609.

Predko, Mike *Programming and Customizing the PIC Microcontroller,* McGraw-Hill/TAB Electronics; 3rd edition, 2007, ISBN- 0071472878.

http://datasheets.chipdb.org/Signetics/2650/2650UM.pdf

Computer Architecture, General

Augarten, Stan, State of the Art, 1983, Ticknor & Fields, ISBN 0-89919-206-8.

Bell, C. Gordon and Newell, Allen, Computer Structures: Readings and Examples, McGraw Hill Inc., January 1, 1971, ISBN- 0070043574.

Blaauw, Gerrit A. and Brooks, Frederick P. Jr. Computer Architecture, Concepts and Evolution, 2 volumes, 1997, Addison-Wesley, IBN 0-201-10557-8.

Bryant, Randal E. and O'Hallaron, David R. Computer Systems: A Programmer's Perspective, 2nd edition, Addison Wesley, Kindle e-book edition, ASIN: B004S81RXE.

Boole, George An Investigation of the Laws of Thought on which are Founded the Mathematical Theories of Logic and Probability, 1854, reprinted 1958, Dover, ISBN 0-48660028-9.

Burks, Arthur; W. Goldstein, Herman H.; Von Neumann, John Preliminary Discussion of the Logical Design of an Electronic Computing Instrument, 1987, MIT Press, originally published in Papers of John Von Neumann on Computing and Computer Theory.

Carter, Nick Schaum's Outline of Computer Architecture, McGraw-Hill; 1st edition (December 26, 2001) ISBN-007136207X.

Comer, Douglas E. Essentials of Computer Architecture, Prentice Hall; US Ed edition (August 23, 2004) ISBN 0131491792.

Englander, Irv The Architecture of Computer Hardware and Systems Software: An Information Technology Approach, Wiley; 3 edition (January 20, 2003) ISBN-0471073253.

Flores, Ivan The Logic of Computer Arithmetic, 1963, Prentice-Hall, ISBN 0135400392.

Harris, David and Harris, Sarah Digital Design and Computer Architecture, Morgan Kaufmann (March 2, 2007) ISBN 012370497.9

Hennessy, John L. and Patterson, David A. Computer Architecture, Fifth Edition: A Quantitative Approach, Morgan Kaufmann; (September 30, 2011) ISBN 012383872X.

Heuring, Vincent, and Jordan, Harry F. Computer Systems Design and Architecture (2nd Edition), Prentice Hall; 2 edition (December 6, 2003) ISBN 0130484407.

ANSI/IEEE Standard 754-1985 for Binary Floating-Point Arithmetic, IEEE Computer, Jan. 1980.

Kidder, Tracy The Soul of a New Machine, Back Bay Books (June 2000) ISBN 0316491977.

Mano, M. Morris Computer System Architecture (3rd Edition), Prentice Hall; 3rd edition (October 29, 1992) ISBN 0131755633.

Murdocca, Miles J. and Heuring, Vincent Computer Architecture and Organization: An Integrated Approach, Wiley (March 16, 2007) ISBN 0471733881.

Nisan, Noam and Schocken, Shimon, The Elements of Computing Systems: Building a Modern Computer from First Principles, 2005, MIT Press, ISBN 0262640686.

Null, Linda The Essentials of Computer Organization And Architecture, Jones & Bartlett Pub; 2 edition (February 15, 2006) ISBN 0763737690.

Page, Daniel, A Practical Introduction to Computer Architecture, 2009, Springer, ISBN 1848822553.

Patterson, David A and Hennessy, John L. Computer Organization and Design: The Hardware/Software Interface, Revised Fourth Edition, Morgan Kaufmann; Nov. 2011 ISBN 0123744938.

Ramachandran, Umakishore, and Leahy William D. Jr., Computer Systems: An Integrated Approach to Architecture and Operating Systems, 2010, Addison Wesley, ISBN 0321486137.

Reid, T. R. The Chip: How Two Americans Invented the Microchip and Launched a Revolution, Random House Trade Paperbacks; Revised edition (October 9, 2001) ISBN 0375758283.

Richards, R. K. Arithmetic Operations in Digital Computers, 1955, Van Nostrand, B00128Z00.

Schmid, Hermann Decimal Computation, 1974, Wiley, ISBN 0-471-76180-X.

Shriver, Bruce D. The Anatomy of a High-Performance Microprocessor: A Systems Perspective, Wiley-IEEE Computer Society Press (June 4, 1998) ISBN 0818684003.

Silc, Jurji, Robic, Borut, Ungerer, Theo Processor Architecture: FROM Dataflow to Superscalar and Beyond, Springer; 1st edition (July 20, 1999) ISBN 3540647988.

Slater, Michael Microprocessor-Based Design A Comprehensive Guide to Effective Hardware Design, 1989, Prentice Hall, ISBN 0-13-582248-3.

Stakem, Patrick H. A Practitioner's Guide to RISC Microprocessor Architecture, Wiley-Interscience (April 12, 1996) ISBN 0471130184.

Stallings, William Computer Organization and Architecture: Designing for Performance (7th Edition), Prentice Hall; 7 edition (July 21, 2005) ISBN 0131856448.

Stokes, Jon, Inside the Machine An Illustrated Introduction to Microprocessors and Computer Architecture, 2006, No Starch Press, ISBN 1593271042.

Resources

wikipedia, various. Material from Wikipedia (www.wikipedia.org) is used under the conditions of the Creative commons Attribution-ShareAlike #.0 Unported License. http://creativecommons.org/licenses/by-sa/3,0

http://www.intel.com/content/www/us/en/company-overview/intel-museum.html

www.antiquetech.com

www.CPU-world.com

www.CPUshack.com

www.happytrees.org/chips CPU graveyard

http://landley.net/history/mirror/tech/processors/CPU.html#tableofcontents

http://www.ibm.com/developerworks/library/pa-microhist.html.

http://www.6502.org

http://klabs.org/

http://www.CPU-collection.de

Scientific American, May 1975, entire issue on Mciroprocessors.

"A Short History of Microprocessors,"
http://www.s100computers.com/History.htm

http://www.hpmuseum.org/

www.bitsavers.org

http://datasheets.chipdb.org/

Patents

There are a large number of microelectronics patents, way too many to list. Browsing them online at the Patent Office site (http://patft.uspto.gov/), or via Google Patents (www.google.com/patents) gives a nice chronological view of who was doing what, when.

This is a good place to start: 4,074,351 Boone, et al (Texas Instruments) Variable function programmed calculator, Feb. 24, 1977.

If you enjoyed this book, you might also be interested in some of these.

16-bit Microprocessors, History and Architecture, 2013 PRRB Publishing, ISBN-1520210922.

4- and 8-bit Microprocessors, Architecture and History, 2013, PRRB Publishing, ISBN-152021572X,

Apollo's Computers, 2014, PRRB Publishing, ISBN-1520215800.

The Architecture and Applications of the ARM Microprocessors, 2013, PRRB Publishing, ISBN-1520215843.

Earth Rovers: for Exploration and Environmental Monitoring, 2014, PRRB Publishing, ISBN-152021586X.

Embedded Computer Systems, Volume 1, Introduction and Architecture, 2013, PRRB Publishing, ISBN-1520215959.

The History of Spacecraft Computers from the V-2 to the Space Station, 2013, PRRB Publishing, ISBN-1520216181.

Floating Point Computation, 2013, PRRB Publishing, ISBN-152021619X.

Architecture of Massively Parallel Microprocessor Systems, 2011, PRRB Publishing, ISBN-1520250061.

Multicore Computer Architecture, 2014, PRRB Publishing, ISBN-1520241372.

Personal Robots, 2014, PRRB Publishing, ISBN-1520216254.

RISC Microprocessors, History and Overview, 2013, PRRB Publishing, ISBN-1520216289.

*Robots and Telerobots in Space Application*s, 2011, PRRB Publishing, ISBN-1520210361.

The Saturn Rocket and the Pegasus Missions, 1965, 2013, PRRB Publishing, ISBN-1520209916.

Visiting the NASA Centers, and Locations of Historic Rockets & Spacecraft, 2017, PRRB Publishing, ISBN-1549651205.

Microprocessors in Space, 2011, PRRB Publishing, ISBN-1520216343.

Computer *Virtualization and the Cloud,* 2013, PRRB Publishing, ISBN-152021636X.

What's the Worst That Could Happen? Bad Assumptions, Ignorance, Failures and Screw-ups in Engineering Projects, 2014, PRRB Publishing, ISBN-1520207166.

Computer Architecture & Programming of the Intel x86 Family, 2013, PRRB Publishing, ISBN-1520263724.

The Hardware and Software Architecture of the Transputer, 2011,PRRB Publishing, ISBN-152020681X.

Mainframes, Computing on Big Iron, 2015, PRRB Publishing, ISBN- 1520216459.

Spacecraft Control Centers, 2015, PRRB Publishing, ISBN-1520200617.

Embedded in Space, 2015, PRRB Publishing, ISBN-1520215916.

A Practitioner's Guide to RISC Microprocessor Architecture, Wiley-Interscience, 1996, ISBN-0471130184.

Cubesat Engineering, PRRB Publishing, 2017, ISBN-1520754019.

Cubesat Operations, PRRB Publishing, 2017, ISBN-152076717X.

Interplanetary Cubesats, PRRB Publishing, 2017, ISBN-1520766173 .

Cubesat Constellations, Clusters, and Swarms, Stakem, PRRB Publishing, 2017, ISBN-1520767544.

Graphics Processing Units, an overview, 2017, PRRB Publishing, ISBN-1520879695.

Intel Embedded and the Arduino-101, 2017, PRRB Publishing, ISBN-1520879296.

Orbital Debris, the problem and the mitigation, 2018, PRRB Publishing, ISBN-*1980466483*.

Manufacturing in Space, 2018, PRRB Publishing, ISBN-1977076041.

NASA's Ships and Planes, 2018, PRRB Publishing, ISBN-1977076823.

Space Tourism, 2018, PRRB Publishing, ISBN-1977073506.

STEM – Data Storage and Communications, 2018, PRRB Publishing, ISBN-1977073115.

In-Space Robotic Repair and Servicing, 2018, PRRB Publishing, ISBN-1980478236.

Introducing Weather in the pre-K to 12 Curricula, A Resource Guide for Educators, 2017, PRRB Publishing, ISBN-1980638241.

Introducing Astronomy in the pre-K to 12 Curricula, A Resource Guide for Educators, 2017, PRRB Publishing, ISBN-198104065X.

Also available in a Brazilian Portuguese edition, ISBN-1983106127.

Deep Space Gateways, the Moon and Beyond, 2017, PRRB Publishing, ISBN-1973465701.

Exploration of the Gas Giants, Space Missions to Jupiter, Saturn, Uranus, and Neptune, PRRB Publishing, 2018, ISBN-9781717814500.

Crewed Spacecraft, 2017, PRRB Publishing, ISBN-1549992406.

Rocketplanes to Space, 2017, PRRB Publishing, ISBN-1549992589.

Crewed Space Stations, 2017, PRRB Publishing, ISBN-1549992228.

Enviro-bots for STEM: Using Robotics in the pre-K to 12 Curricula, A Resource Guide for Educators, 2017, PRRB Publishing, ISBN-1549656619.

STEM-Sat, Using Cubesats in the pre-K to 12 Curricula, A Resource Guide for Educators, 2017, ISBN-1549656376.

Embedded GPU's, 2018, PRRB Publishing, ISBN-1980476497.

Mobile Cloud Robotics, 2018, PRRB Publishing, ISBN-1980488088.

Extreme Environment Embedded Systems, 2017, PRRB Publishing, ISBN-1520215967.

What's the Worst, Volume-2, 2018, ISBN-1981005579.

Spaceports, 2018, ISBN-1981022287.

Space Launch Vehicles, 2018, ISBN-1983071773.

Mars, 2018, ISBN-1983116902.

X-86, 40th Anniversary ed, 2018, ISBN-1983189405.

Lunar Orbital Platform-Gateway, 2018, PRRB Publishing, ISBN-1980498628.

Space Weather, 2018, ISBN-1723904023.

STEM-Engineering Process, 2017, ISBN-1983196517.

Space Telescopes, 2018, PRRB Publishing, ISBN-1728728568.

Exoplanets, 2018, PRRB Publishing, ISBN-9781731385055.

Planetary Defense, 2018, PRRB Publishing, ISBN-9781731001207.

Exploration of the Asteroid Belt, 2018, PRRB Publishing, ISBN-1731049846.

Terraforming, 2018, PRRB Publishing, ISBN-1790308100.

Martian Railroad, 2019, PRRB Publishing, ISBN-1794488243.

Exoplanets, 2019, PRRB Publishing, ISBN-1731385056.

Exploiting the Moon, 2019, PRRB Publishing, ISBN-1091057850.

RISC-V, an Open Source Solution for Space Flight Computers, 2019, PRRB Publishing, ISBN-1796434388.

Arm in Space, 2019, PRRB Publishing, ISBN-9781099789137.

Search for *Extraterrestrial Life*, 2019, PRRB Publishing, ISBN-978-1072072188.

Submarine Launched Ballistic Missiles, 2019, ISBN-978-1088954904.

Space Command, Military in Space, 2019, PRRB Publishing, ISBN-978-1693005398.

Robotic Exploration of the Icy moons of the Gas Giants, ISBN- 979-8621431006.

History & Future of Cubesats, ISBN-978-1986536356.

Robtic Exploration of the Icy Moons of the Ice Giants, by Swarms of Cubesats, ISBN-979-8621431006.

Swarm Robotics, ISBN-979-8534505948.

Introduction to Electric Power Systems, ISBN-979-8519208727.

Powerships, Powerbarges, Floating Wind Farms: electricity when and where you need it, 2021, PRRB ‍blishing, ISBN-979-8716199477.

‍ntros de Control: Operaciones en Satélites del ‍stándar CubeSat (Spanish Edition), 2021, ISBN-979-8510113068.

The Artemis Missions, Return to the Moon, and on to Mars, 2021, ISBN-979-8490532361.

James Webb Space Telescope. A New Era in Astronomy, 2021, ISBN-979-8773857969.

www.ingramcontent.com/pod-product-compliance
Lightning Source LLC
Chambersburg PA
CBHW031222050326
40689CB00009B/1441